Your Towns and Cities

Dartford

in the Great War

Your Towns and Cities in the Great War

Dartford

in the Great War

by Stephen Wynn

Pen & Sword
MILITARY

First published in Great Britain in 2016 by
PEN & SWORD MILITARY
an imprint of
Pen and Sword Books Ltd
47 Church Street
Barnsley
South Yorkshire S70 2AS

ISBN 978 1 47382 7 905

A CIP record for this book is available from the British Library

Printed and bound in England
by CPI Group (UK) Ltd, Croydon, CR0 4YY

Pen & Sword Books Ltd incorporates the imprints of
Pen & Sword Archaeology, Atlas, Aviation, Battleground, Discovery,
Family History, History, Maritime, Military, Naval, Politics, Railways,
Select, Social History, Transport, True Crime, and Claymore Press,
Frontline Books, Leo Cooper, Praetorian Press, Remember When,
Seaforth Publishing and Wharncliffe.

For a complete list of Pen and Sword titles please contact
Pen and Sword Books Limited
47 Church Street, Barnsley, South Yorkshire, S70 2AS, England
E-mail: enquiries@pen-and-sword.co.uk
Website: www.pen-and-sword.co.uk

Contents

'The journey to the trenches was rather nauseating – Dead men's legs sticking through the sides with puttees and boots still on – Bits of bones and skull with hair peeled off and tons of equipment and clothing lying about. This sort of thing together with the strong stench and the dead and mangled body of the pilot, combined to upset me for a few days.'

Major Edward Mannock VC DSO MC – 85 Squadron RFC
(On arriving at an enemy aircraft he had just shot down)

Acknowledgements

Many thanks to my wife Tanya for her continual support and for providing photographs and documentation for the compilation of this book. Thanks also to Andrew Bratley for allowing me to use his research concerning men from Dartford in Kent who served with Australian Forces during the war and who were killed.

CHAPTER ONE

A Brief History of Dartford

Dartford has a long and varied history beginning in early medieval times when it became a market town which, besides the local population, brought with it a transient population of pilgrims and travellers on their way to Canterbury and beyond. Some of them liked what they found and stayed which resulted in diversity in both religion and culture. Today it has a thriving community which has resulted in Dartford being granted borough status.

Dartford Museum, Library and War Memorial (Wikipedia)

Archaeological evidence shows that the area was first populated some 250,000 years ago. Over the years it has had Roman, Saxon as well as Norman influences. It was mentioned in the Domesday Book in the form of Dartford Manor.

Various religious orders settled in the town, including the Knights Templars. During the Peasants Revolt of 1381 groups of rebels met here before marching to both Canterbury and London to vent their frustration. A local pub is named Tylers after one of the peasants' leaders, a man by the name of Wat Tyler.

The town has had its fair share of connections with royalty over the years. As far back as 1415, King Henry V, en route to fighting the French at the Battle of Agincourt, marched through the town with his army. When he died suddenly just seven years later on 31 August 1422, his body travelled through Dartford on its way to Westminster Abbey and a state funeral. In 1452 the Duke of York, with an army of 10,000 men, was encamped on Dartford Brent, a large expanse of common land on the outskirts of the town, before he surrendered to King Henry VI. A hundred years later in 1555, the same location was the setting for the burning at the stake of a local Protestant, Christopher Ward.

Anne of Cleves, the fourth wife of Henry VIII, lived in Dartford for a while after their marriage was annulled on 9 July 1540.

Dartford Grammar School, which lost some of its young sons during the fighting of the First World War, was founded in 1576.

When it comes to industry, the town has certainly had a varied history. Over the years it has ranged from agriculture, brewing, lime burning, chalk mining, a paper mill, engineering, a gunpowder factory and even the manufacture of mustard.

The outbreak of the First World War saw the town's population at just over 40,000. With massive numbers of men needed to go off and fight, a brisk increase in trade for the local Vickers factory, and the country's largest pharmaceutical company in the form of Burroughs-Wellcome Chemical Works, those of working age would all be required in some capacity.

Along with London and numerous other towns that were situated across the south of the country, Dartford saw the arrival of large numbers of Belgian refugees, who had managed to escape the full force of what appeared to be an ever advancing German Army.

CHAPTER TWO

Dartford Grammar School
War Memorial

Dartford Grammar School was founded in 1576 and today has well over 1,000 pupils on its roll. Its current location in Shepherds Lane, at the top of West Hill, is one of several sites where the school has been located since it started out in the High Street above the Corn Market House, a building which sadly has long since been demolished.

The school has its very own ornately carved roll of honour to

Dartford Grammar School War Memorial

commemorate its 'Old Boys' who were killed during the First World War. There are forty-six names on it and the following inscription.

Dartford Grammar School
Roll of Remembrance of Old Boys
who gave their lives for their country
1914 – 1918

Those commemorated are listed below; and I will look at some of those who are named on it, in more detail.

Allen, Hubert C.	Lloyd, Valentine
Apps, Reginald D.	Ludlow, Herbert
Ashton, Cyril J.	Manley, Hamilton D.
Baker, Victor S.	Monkman, Fred K.
Bare, Cecil L.	Mosley, Harold D.
Birch, William T.	Nicholas, Paul H.
Bloomfield, Leonard	Palmer, Harry H.
Bloomfield, Sidney.	Peerless, Neville
Bowers, Frank E.	Plant, Percy W.
Brown, Edward C.	Pocock, William H.
Bradley, C. Raymond.	Raynor, B. Harold
Brown, J. Ferguson.	Sanders, William F.
Clay, Walter J.	Schrivener, Arthur W.
Chatterton, William T.	Sharp, Humphrey
Davis, J. Frederick.	Smith, John D.M.
Dodd, Francis C.	Smith, Percival T.
Dowsett, Henry C	Smith, W. Leslie
Fry, Horace C.	Stephen, Norman V.
Harris, Sydney E.	Summers, Gordon W.
Inkpen, Wilfred	Tucker, Harold G.
Humphries, William C.	Walton, L. Maitland.
Johnson, H. Ernest	Whatley, H. Albert
Kerr, William	Wiggens, Frank W.

Second Lieutenant Reginald Denman Apps enlisted in the army early on in the war and was commissioned into the 1st Battalion, Princess Charlotte of Wales's (Royal Berkshire) Regiment. He was killed in action on 17 May 1915 during fighting at the Battle of

Festubert, which was a British attack on German positions in the Artois region of France. The planned infantry assault was preceded by a sixty-hour artillery bombardment of German lines by 100,000 shells, which failed significantly to damage the front line defences of the German Sixth Army. Ultimately the offensive was successful and Festubert was captured by the British, but their efforts came at a cost of some 16,648 casualties. Reginald Denman Apps was one of them.

His name is commemorated on the War Memorial at Le Touret, in the Pas de Calais region of France. The memorial includes the names of over 13,000 British soldiers who were killed in the area from October 1914 until late September 1915 and who have no known grave.

According to the 1911 Census, Reginald lived at 12 The Court, Bury Fields, Guildford, Surrey with his parents, Benjamin Charles and Mary Florence Apps, and his younger brother, John Pollington Apps. Even though Reginald was only 17 years of age he was thought trustworthy and bright enough to be the Clerk to the District Valuer, an important role for one so young.

Second Lieutenant Wilfred Inkpen was born in Dartford in 1898 and, according to the 1911 Census, lived at 20 Nelson Road, Dartford. His parents, Thomas and Minnie Inkpen, had six other children: George, Ernest, Percy, Albert, Elsie and Dorothy.

Wilfred enlisted in the army and at the time of his death on 26 October 1917 he was a temporary second lieutenant in the 2nd Battalion of the Border Regiment. His name is commemorated on the Tyne Cot War Memorial at Zonnebeke, near Ypres in Belgium.

The 2nd Battalion was raised in August 1914 in Pembroke Dock and became part of the 7th Division, 20 Brigade. By 6 October 1914 they had landed at Zeebrugge and they remained on the Western Front until November 1917, when they were moved to the Italian Front. They took part in the later stages of the Battle of Passchendaele, which began on 26 October 1917, the day on which Wilfred was killed in action.

I can find no definitive records of Wilfred's four brothers having served during the First World War, although it is highly unlikely that they did not. There were five men with the name Albert Inkpen, five George Inkpens, three Ernest Inkpens and three Percy Inkpens who all served in the British Army during the First World War.

Private Herbert Leonard Ernest Ludlow (24202) of the 2nd Battalion, The Grenadier Guards, was killed in action on 25 September 1916, aged 19. He was born in the nearby village of Sutton-at-Hone.

The only son and child of Arthur and Florence Mary Ludlow, in the 1911 Census the family were living at 19 The Brent, Dartford, where Arthur was the steward at the local Conservative Club. After the war they moved to 5 Knockhall Road, Greenhithe, Kent.

Although Herbert is buried at The Guards' Cemetery at Lesboeufs in France, he is also remembered on his mother's headstone in the cemetery of St John the Baptist Church in Sutton-at-Hone. She died on 15 March 1924 aged 54.

The 2nd Battalion of the Grenadier Guards arrived in France on 15 August 1914, less than two weeks after the start of hostilities and remained there for the remainder of the war, taking part in numerous battles across the Western Front. The war diaries show that they were in trenches near the Ginchy-les-Boeufs road, in what became the Battle of Morval, and records the following entry for 25 September 1916. The first entry is timed 12.35pm, zero hour at the start of the battle.

> *'Trenches were narrow – men shoulder-to-shoulder, unable to sit down. 12.35pm – own barrage opened and battalion advanced in two waves of two companies each. It seemed that the Germans knew of the attacks as they shelled heavily within a minute of the advance. The wire had not been cut by the artillery and ways had to be found to cut through it in the face of heavy fire.*
> *1.35pm - Moved forward to edge of village of Les Boeufs.*
> *2.35pm – Marched through the village and gained eastern end. The new position was shelled by the Germans during the evening.'*

Second Lieutenant Fred Kerebey Monkman of the 26th Battalion, Royal Fusiliers, died of his wounds on 28 September 1917 during the Third Battle of Ypres at Polygon Wood. The Royal Fusiliers, who were also known as the City of London Regiment, raised an amazing seventy-six battalions during the First World War. The 26th Battalion was also known as the 'bankers' battalion because the men who enlisted in it came from the clerks and accountants of the City of London's banks. It was raised by the Lord Mayor of London on 17 May 1915 and first landed in France on 4 May 1916.

Lieutenant Monkman is buried at the Lijssenthoek Military Cemetery, Poperinghe in Belgium. During the war the village of Lijssenthoek was part of the journey Allied troops had to make when travelling between the battlefields at Ypres at the front and the military bases that were situated a safe distance to the rear, putting them just

Lijssentoek Military Cemetery – Commonwealth War Graves Commission

out of reach of the German artillery.

The cemetery was first used by Commonwealth forces in June 1915, mainly because of the Casualty Clearing Station which was situated nearby.

The 1901 Census showed Fred living with his parents, William and Emily Monkman, along with his sister May and his elder brother Monty, at 94 Oak View, Shipley, Horsham in Sussex. By the time of the 1911 Census the family had moved to 35 Highfield Road, Dartford and Fred had another brother, Roy, who was 9 years old. Fred, who was 17, at the time, is not shown as living with the family.

Captain Arthur William Scrivener MC, 1st/10th Battalion, London Regiment was a holder of the Military Cross. He was killed on 2 November 1917 at the age of 23 and is buried at the Gaza War Cemetery. At the time of his death Arthur was involved in the Third Battle of Gaza, that took place between 27 October and 7 November 1917 and resulted in the capture of the ruined city by Allied forces.

According to the 1911 Census, Arthur, who was an only child, was 16 years old, still at school, and lived with his widowed mother, Edith, her sister Eleanor and a general servant also named Edith, at 'Rostrevor', Sandhurst Road, Sidcup in Kent.

CHAPTER THREE

Dartford War Memorial

Dartford set up a War Memorial Committee to determine how the town would commemorate its dead from the Great War. They agreed on a design and chose Arthur George Walker as their sculptor, after seeing the memorial he had produced for the nearby town of Sevenoaks, which also has a British soldier as its main feature. The story goes that he met a soldier home on leave whom he sketched and then made the sculpture from his drawings. The identity of the soldier was sadly not recorded, but according to Walker himself, the man survived the war to see photographs of the finished statue.

Walker was a renowned British sculptor and painter of his day, with his best known works being the statue of Florence Nightingale at Waterloo Place in London and the war memorial in Derby. He was also responsible for war memorials in twelve other towns and cities across the UK. The Dartford War Memorial is in the form of a granite pedestal on a base of the same material. On top of these proudly sits the bronze statue of a British soldier.

There are seven inscriptions

Dartford War Memorial.

included on the memorial as it includes the names of those men from the town who fell in subsequent conflicts. The one which relates directly to the First World War reads as follows:

'In grateful memory of the gallant sons of this town, who fell in the fight for freedom 1914-1919'

The Dartford War Memorial was unveiled by Air Vice Marshal Sir William Geoffrey Hanson Salmond on 7 May 1922. Sir Geoffrey, as he was always known, had been a senior commander in the Royal Flying Corps, remaining in service after the war in the Royal Air Force. On 1 April 1933 he took over the position of Chief of the Air Staff from his brother John. Four days later on 5 April, John resumed the role after Geoffrey was taken ill with what turned out to be incurable cancer. He died on 27 April 1933.

Ackland, C.	Blackmore, F.C.	Chacksfield, H.G
Ager, W.J.	Blanks, L.	Chadwick, A.
Allen, H.G.	Blowers, H.W.V.	Challis, S.W.
Archer, E.	Bloxham, A.J.	Chambers, F.B.
Archer, R.	Board, F.G.	Cheeseman, N.W.F.
Ashby, R.	Bodycomb, A.G.	Clarke, T.
Attenbury, J.	Bodycomb, G.T.	Clarke, J.T.
Baker, V.S.	Booker, E.P.	Coad, R.H.
Balchin, F	Booker, T.	Cocup, R.M.
Ballard, W.J.	Boudrie, E.A	Cocup, W.T.
Barden, H.	Bowler, E.J.	Colley, J H.
Barker, S.J	Bowles, S.	Collins, J.B.
Barnes, F.	Bragg, H.G	Collins, P.J.
Barton, A.	Brookes, A.	Colyer, G.
Bass, A.J	Brooks, W.	Cooper, A.
Bates, T.H.	Browning, J.	Cooper, C.
Baulk, E.H.	Buckley, J.	Cooper, W.A.L.
Baulk, H.P	Burgess, W.H	Couchman, A. E.
Belchambers, G.J.	Button, A.W.	Cox, A.E.
Bird, E.	Carey, W.D.	Cox, E.
Black, A.J.	Carpenter, A.E	Cox, P.
Blackman, S.H.	Carr, A.	Crickenham, H.
Blackman, S.J.H.	Carter, G.L.	Crowhurst, J.T.

Crowhurst, S.G.
Crowhurst, W.R.
Cuckow, E.T.
Dando, W.B.
Darville, P.L
Davies, E.J.
Davis, J.B.
Day, A.
Day, C.W.
Dickens, C.S.
Dixon, E.F.
Dixon, F.J.
Dixon, G.
Dixon, S.G
Donovan, J.
Downes, E.
Duncan, J.
Dyde, P.S.
Earley, W.
Easter, J.J.
Engley, K.
Essex, P.G.
Everson, H.T.
Exeter, A.T.
Farr, F.J.
Farrow, H.
Faulks, E.
Fender, G.H.
Fish, A.
Flint, F.D.
Florence, W.J.
Franklin, C.T.
Free, G.
Free, W.
Fricker, G.
Fryer, G.W.
Fullegar, G.H.

Fuller, F.E.
Gardiner, J.W.
Garner, E.L.
Gausden, J.F.
George, J.A.
Giles, E.W.
Gold, W.J
Golding, W.T.
Goodhew, A.H.
Gould, P.J.
Gray, S.C.
Gregory, W.A.
Gregory, W.J.
Greig, R.M.J.
Griffin, H.J.
Hall, E.
Hall, J.
Hall, S.
Hampton, A.
Hanlon, L.W.
Harber, B.A.
Harden, S.V.
Harding, A.J.
Hargreaves, J.H.
Hate, W.T.
Hawkins, R.W.
Haygreen, C.
Haygreen, E.H.
Henry, F.
Heron, T.
Hicks, A.M
Hicks, J.G.
Hicks, T.H.
Hickson, G.H.
Higgins, J.G.
Hill, H.W.
Hills, A.

Hills, G.H.
Hodge, F.
Hodge, W.T.
Hodsdon, A.E.
Hodsdon, W.
Holton, A.
Hopkins, A.H.
Horning, C.F.
Howells, J.
Hughes, F.
Hulks, E.W.N.
Humble, G.
Humphrey, A S.
Humphrey, G.
Hunt, A.H.
Hunt, C.G.
Huntley, D.
Inkpen, W.
Johnson, W.H.
Jones, D.S.W.
Kember, L.J.
Kerr, W.
Keyes, C.
Kirk, R.
Knapp, F.
Knott, R.A.
Kemp, T.
Lander, W.H.
Laurel, I.
Laurie, W.
Lawrence, C.E.
Leach, B.
Leach, P.
Lee, G.L.
Lewis, D.E.
Lewis, G.
Lucas, A.

Ludlow, H.L.E.
Luker, A.
Lusted, B.A.
Lynds, H.J.
Lynn, J.
Mackerness, A.
Mackerness, C.
Mackintosh, J.S.
Manley, H.D.
Mann, C.
Manser, D.H.
Martin, C.H.
Martin, G.J.
Martin, H.
Martin, J.A.W.
Martin, W.
Maxted, C.E.
May, A.
May, E.
May, E.F.
May, F.C.
May, G.
May, F.
May, J.
May, W.E.
Miller, A.A.
Miller, S.T.
Mills, C.P.
Mitchell, J.E.
Mitchell, L.
Mitchell, M.
Mitchell, S.M.
Monkman, F.K.
Moss, A.C.
Moyes, W.
Nash, S.
Newman, W.A.

Norkett, A.M.
Oaten, H.J.
O'Connor, T.
Odell, W.M.
Oliver, N.W.C.
Oliver, S.A.
Oliver, S.S.
Oliver, T.
Oliver, N.H.
Oram, A.J.
Orton, G.E.
Ould, W.F.
Outram, G.H.
Parker, C.G.
Parris, R.
Pavelin, W.
Payne, A.G.
Pearmain, A.E.
Peerless, A.N.
Pelly, C.
Perry, J.
Peters, J.T.
Piggott, H.J.
Pipe, A.V.
Pocock, S.A.
Poffley, G.A.
Poile, G.R.
Porter, E.E.
Potter, W.
Powell, W.
Powles, C.F.
Prime, L.S.
Prue, H.
Pullen, W.
Rafter, J.
Ravenor, P.R.
Rayner, B.H.

Read, G.W.
Reardon, F.
Reed, J.
Reeves, A.
Reeves, T.
Reid, G.J.
Richardson, J.A.
Ridgewell, H.G.
Ridgewell, J.L.
Roberts, G.
Roberts, J.
Robertson, A.
Robinson, A.W.
Robinson, F.S.
Rowlstone, R.
Russell, E.G.
Sales, A.G.
Saxby, E.J.
Scott, T.R.
Scudamore, C.
Searing, G.T.
Searles, E.R.
Sharpe, T.
Shaw, G.A.
Sheeran, E.
Shirley, S.J.
Shrubb, C.
Shuttle, C.H.N.
Sims, J.E.
Sinden, A.
Small, H.E.
Small H.E. (Jnr).
Smith, A.C.
Smith, G.J.
Smith, P.T.
Snelling, R.A.
Solomons, A.

Spendiff, W.R.	Tomalin, A.J.	West, A.E.V.
Stevens, C.	Tompkins, G.P.	Whatley, A.
Stevens, E.	Tucker, H.G	Whiting, H.E.
Stevens, J.W.	Tucker, L.H.	Wilkins, C.J.
Stevens, W.	Tungate, A.E.	Willett, F.M.
Stokes, S.	Turley, W.	Wilsher, A.S.B.
Stone, J.	Turner, A.H.	Wise, F.B.
Stoneham, L.	Turner, C.R.C.	Wood, F.J.
Street, F.G.	Walker, H.J.C.	Wood, W.I.J.
Sullivan, W.	Walker, J.T.F.	Woodgate, E.C.
Summers, W.G.	Waller, H.W.	Wooding, R.
Sutton, C.	Wallis, A.	Woods, J.W.
Symons, H.	Warren, G.D.	Woolley, C.C.T.
Talbot, A.H.	Waters, A.T.	Wright, T.H.
Tatner, G.	Wenham, E.E.	Wykes, J.R.
Thompson, F.C.	Wenham, F.V.	Young, J.F.
Thrussell, F.C.	Westborn, J.P.	

Gunner Walter Thomas Pavelin (67051) 6th Battery, Royal Field Artillery was killed during the retreat from the Battle of Mons on 26 August 1914. He was 19 years old. He was born at Dartford in 1895 and enlisted at nearby Woolwich and had only been in France for a week before he was killed.

His name is commemorated on the La Ferté-sous-Jouarre Memorial which records the names of some 3,740 officers and men who fell at the Battle of Mons but who have no known grave. The memorial was unveiled on 4 November 1928 by Sir William Pulteney who had been the commander of the British Expeditionary Force's 3 Corps in 1914.

In just over two weeks leading up to the end of August 1914, the German Army had almost reached Paris, having successfully invaded Belgium and then pushed on through northern France, forcing British and French troops to retreat in their path.

The 1911 Census showed that Walter lived at 16 St Albans Road, Dartford, with his parents Thomas and Clara Pavelin and his four siblings: William, Thomas, Winifred and Lilian. Walter's parents Thomas and Clara both worked at a local gun and shell factory, producing munitions for the war effort. This was possibly the Vickers and Halls Munitions factory in Dartford, where Thomas would have been paid more than his wife for doing exactly the same work. In 1917 Dartford's munitions workers took industrial action, which would have greatly affected production.

Farrier Sergeant Ernest Henry Baulk (686831), 'B' Battery, 293 Brigade, Royal Field Artillery died two days after the war's end at 10.30am on 13 November 1918 at Fort Pitt Hospital in Chatham. He was 29 years old.

Ernest was given a full military funeral, but only after his brother William requested it. The ceremony took place on 20 November 1918 at Dartford's East Hill Cemetery where there are twenty-six other graves of British servicemen from the First World War.

East Hill Cemetery, Dartford. (Commonwealth War Graves Commission)

When Ernest enlisted in the army on 27 October 1915 his home address was shown as 140 Western Terrace, Dartford Road, Dartford. He arrived in France on 7 February 1917, staying there until 17 March 1918. He returned home for two weeks leave before returning on 2 April 1918 where he stayed until 6 November 1918. He arrived back in the UK the next day and six days later died from asthma and bronchitis, having contracted influenza on 2 November.

Although every death during the war was tinged with sadness, Ernest's must have been particularly difficult for his family to deal with. Having survived the horrors of the war, which he had been involved in for eighteen months, with only a two week break, he then died after the war had finished, the victim of an illness. His death was particularly hard on his sister Edith, who was his next of kin. His brother, William Baulk, lived at 7 Dartford Road, Whitehill Estate, Dartford.

Besides William and Edith, Ernest had two other brothers, Charles and George and another sister, Emily. By the time of the 1911 Census, his mother, also Emily, was a patient at the Holborn Union Workhouse Infirmary in Upper Holloway, North London. When she entered the workhouse is not known but she was not shown as living with the family on the previous 1901 Census.

Charles Baulk had served as a private (991) with the 2nd Battalion, Royal West Kent Regiment during the war, enlisting at Gravesend on 23 September 1914. By the time he had finished his training it was 9 December 1915. He served in India between 8 April 1916 and 22 April 1917. He then went to Mesopotamia as part of the Expeditionary Force where he stayed until 31 December 1918 before starting his journey back to the UK on New Year's Day 1919.

After the war he was demobbed at Hounslow on 25 March 1919 and was living at 15 Gloucester Road, Dartford, with his wife Jessie and their two children, Thomas and Winifred.

The British Army Medal Rolls Index Cards show two William Baulks who served during the war, one with the Queen's (Royal West Surrey) Regiment, Royal Fusiliers and the other with the Royal Engineers. There is no information which allows us with any degree of certainty to confirm whether either of them is the William Baulks we are looking for.

Corporal Charlie Haygreen (54143), 22nd Heavy Battery, Royal Garrison Artillery, died of wounds on 10 October 1917 aged 27. He is buried at the Godewaersvelde British Cemetery in the Nord region of France close to the Belgium border. The cemetery contains 972 Commonwealth graves from the First World War.

Before the war he was a gardener and lived at Little Wickham

Cottage, Fawkham, near Longfield in Kent with his parents, Charles and Emma Haygreen, his sister, Emma, and his two younger brothers, Walter and Ernest.

Walter (John) Haygreen also served in the war as a gunner (54144) with the Royal Garrison Artillery, enlisting just before his twenty-first birthday on 23 November 1914 in Deptford. He survived the war and was demobbed early in 1919.

Younger brother **Ernest (Harry) Haygreen** did not follow in the footsteps of his two brothers into the Royal Garrison Artillery, but instead became a Rifleman (R/28896) in the 2nd/16th Battalion, King's Royal Rifle Corps. Unfortunately, like Charlie, he did not survive the war. He died of his wounds on 28 September 1918, just six weeks before the end of the war whilst serving in France.

Ernest does not have a grave; instead his name has been commemorated on the Tyne Cot War Memorial at Zonnebeke in Belgium.

Lance Corporal Arthur Ernest Tungate (8880), 1st Battalion, Bedfordshire Regiment, was killed in action on 18 April 1915. He was born in Croydon, Surrey in 1889, lived in Dartford and enlisted in Woolwich, London.

The 1901 Census shows Arthur living with his parents, Edwin and Susan Tungate, and his seven brothers and sisters in Camberwell, Surrey. Four of the brothers also served:

Henry James Tungate as a private (6700) in the Coldstream Guards, and arrived in France on 14 August 1914, just ten days after the war had started. He survived the war and lived to the ripe old age of 91 years of age, passing away in Bexley, London in December 1976.

Herbert Charles Tungate was a private in both the Queen's Own (Royal West Kent) Regiment as well as the Buffs (Royal East Kent) Regiment. He also survived the war and died in 1981 aged 88.

Benjamin Tungate served with the East Anglian Field Ambulance, Royal Army Medical Corps. He survived the war and lived to the age of 75, passing away in 1963.

John Harold Tungate, the youngest of the seven brothers, was a sergeant (L/15593) in the 20th Battalion, Duke of Cambridge's Own (Middlesex) Regiment, was awarded the Distinguished Conduct Medal on 2 December 1919. The citation for the award read as follows:

'For marked gallantry and good leadership during the operations of 28th/29th September 1918, on the Ypres-Comines Canal. During the advance to the final objective the company was held up by fire from a concrete pill-box. He rushed forward with his platoon commander, killed the enemy scouts outside the pill-box, and assisted in capturing the entire garrison of thirty men and one machine gun. He then led a portion of his platoon with great dash and daring to the final objective. His fine example of courage inspired all ranks.'

What was even more remarkable about John's feat of outstanding bravery was that he was only 20 years old.

I can find no trace of Arthur's two other brothers, Edwin and Frederick, having served during the First World War, but we know that Edwin passed away in 1960 aged 76 and that Frederick in 1956 aged 58 years of age.

The 1911 Census shows that Arthur was already serving in the army at that time, stationed in Bermuda and Jamaica, but unfortunately his army service record did not survive.

Private Frederick C. Thrussell (3596), 3rd Reserve Regiment, 15th King's Hussars, died on 25 February 1921. He first arrived in France within two weeks of the outbreak of the war on 16 August 1914.

G.H. Fullegar. This man's name has provoked some discussion as it would appear that the name on the Dartford War Memorial might well have been spelt incorrectly. The entry on the memorial is as shown at the beginning of this paragraph.

There is an entry on the Commonwealth War Graves Commission website that shows a George Henry Fullager as a private (GS/873) in the 6th Battalion, Queen's Own (Royal West Kent) Regiment, who was killed on 7 October 1916 and is commemorated on the Thiepval Memorial on the Somme.

The 1911 Census shows a George Henry Fullager aged 22, living at 83 Overy Street, Dartford, with his mother Elizabeth. His job at the time was that of a labourer working in a tannery.

Second Lieutenant George Thomas Bodycomb, Royal Flying Corps, died on 18 February 1918 at Melcombe, near Banbury in Oxfordshire.

In his will he left £272 6s 2d which went to his next of kin, his father Robert Bodycomb.

The 1911 Census showed his home address as 20 Brandon Road, Dartford, where he lived with his parents, Robert and Maria Bodycomb, his brother Sydney and his two sisters Rose and Eva-May. George was only 16 years old at the time and was working as an assistant analytical chemist in an explosives factory. His elder brother Sydney was a carpenter and 25 years old when war broke out in 1914. We could find no trace of a military service record for Sydney, who died in Dartford in 1965 aged 76.

There is another Bodycomb commemorated on the Dartford War Memorial with the initials of A.G. I believe this is **Arthur George Bodycomb** who was George's cousin. Arthur and his brother Herbert both enlisted in the Canadian Army in Toronto; Herbert on 31 March 1915 and Arthur four months later on 31 July 1915. Herbert survived the war.

Private Sidney James Henry Blackman (632258), 20th (County of London) Battalion (Blackheath and Woolwich) London Regiment, died of his wounds in France on 12 January 1917. He was 21 years old and is buried at the Lijssenthoek Military Cemetery in Poperinghe, Belgium. The last action that the 20th Battalion were involved in prior to Sidney's death was the Battle of Transloy which took place between 1 and 18 October 1916.

According to the 1911 Census he lived with his parents, Sidney Herbert and Laura Alice Blackman, along with his four brothers and two sisters at 5 Trevithick Road, Dartford.

The 20th London Battalion have their own website which lists of all those from the battalion who were killed during the First World War, however Sidney is not one of those on the list.

Behind every name on the Dartford War Memorial is a story just waiting to be told; not always just about the named soldier. Often it is about one or more of the man's brothers who also served in the war. It quickly becomes apparent just how many people were affected by the death of a single soldier. Back then many families were large in number, with six or more children not unusual. Often there would be generations of families living in the same communities, which meant cousins and extended family members who might also be married and have children of their own.

I could have written a book purely about the Dartford War Memorial, there are so many names on it. It is also apparent just how many of the men are related to at least one other man named on the memorial. For example there are twenty-five surnames that appear twice, which includes a father and son; seven names that appear three times; two names that appear four times, one of which is the surname Mitchell, where it would appear that three of them were brothers. Another two names appear five times and one surname, that of May, appears eight times.

CHAPTER FOUR

Joyce Green Aerodrome

The aerodrome at Joyce Green did not start out in life as a military airfield. From 1911 it was a testing facility for Vickers Ltd for their prototype aircraft, remembering of course, that the first powered and piloted flight had only taken place on 17 December 1903 when the Wright brothers flew their plane in America.

At the outbreak of war in August 1914 Joyce Green was improved and taken over by the Royal Flying Corps. Hangars were added, along with staff accommodation. As well as being an ideal strategic location to assist with the aerial defence of London, its main function was the final period of training and qualification of new pilots.

One of the base's most famous pilots was Major James Thomas Byford McCudden, who arrived at Joyce Green in March 1917. He was one of the most highly decorated British pilots of the First World War having been awarded the Victoria Cross, the Distinguished Service Order & Bar, the Military Cross & Bar, the Military Medal and the French *Croix de Guerre*.

McCudden was born in Gillingham, Kent on 28 March 1895 into a middle class working family with strong military traditions. He had originally enlisted in the Royal Engineers in 1910 but transferred to the Royal Flying Corps in 1913 where initially he became an observer, not obtaining his pilot's licence until 1916.

When he first arrived in France in August 1914 it was as a mechanic, but he was soon being used as an observer on reconnaissance missions. He won the first of his gallantry awards on 21 January 1916 when he was awarded the *Croix de Guerre* by General Joseph Joffre, who was the commander-in-chief of the French Army. He had previously requested to be able to train as a pilot but had been denied purely because his skills as a mechanic were much needed. However, after being awarded the *Croix de Guerre* he was allowed to return to England to commence pilot training which he passed with 'flying colours', and returned to France on 8 July 1916, joining 20 Squadron.

Major James Thomas Byford McCudden, VC, DSO (Bar), MC (Bar), MM, Croix de Guerre (France).

Two months later in September 1916 he claimed his first victory with his fifth coming in February 1917, officially making him an ace. This resulted in his being awarded both the Military Medal and the Military Cross. He returned to England soon after where he continued to refine his flying skills and train other pilots. He was stationed at Hornchurch Aerodrome at Suttons Farm with 66 Squadron, which at the time was flying the Sopwith Pup aircraft. He transferred to 56 Squadron which was equipped with SE5a fighter aircraft and was achieving success on the Western Front. His score increased during the Third Battle of Ypres and on 6 October 1917 he was awarded a bar to his Military Cross followed two months later by the Distinguished Service Order and Bar. The highest award for valour followed when King George V presented him with the Victoria Cross on 30 March 1918.

McCudden would eventually make a total of fifty-seven confirmed 'kills'; thirty-one of these would come in the last six months of 1917. He was killed, not by an enemy pilot, but in a flying accident on 9 July 1918 in France when his SE5a aircraft crashed following engine failure soon after take-off from Auxi-le-Château.

Another First World War flying ace with connections to Joyce Green Aerodrome is Major Edward Corringham 'Mick' Mannock. He was awarded the Military Cross twice, the Distinguished Service Order on three occasions – an extremely rare achievement – as well as the Victoria Cross, which he was awarded posthumously on 18 July 1919, nearly a year after his death, and only after some intensive lobbying by his former comrades.

Major Edward Corringham 'Mick' Mannock, VC, DSO (Two Bars), MC (Bar).

Aged 31, he was killed in action on 26 July 1918, not shot down by a German flyer, but from ground fire. After shooting down a German LVG two-seater aircraft he flew down low to see the crashed enemy plane, breaking an unwritten rule of what not to do whilst engaged in aerial combat. In doing so he placed himself in shooting range of

German ground troops in nearby trenches, who opened fire on him. His plane caught fire and crashed. His body was never recovered and his name is commemorated on the Flying Corps Memorial, at the Faubourg d'Amiens Cemetery at Arras.

An entry from Mannock's diary goes some way to showing just how un-gentlemanly the life of a pilot actually was. The myth that surrounds flyers of the First World War paints a picture of them as chivalrous and noble knights of the sky flying their machines into battle, with the added bonus of having God on their side. The reality was quite often somewhat different. It was not all about having attended the right school or university, 'jolly hockey sticks', moustaches and 'I say old boy'. Most aerial engagements had a large element of kill or be killed attached to them, even if the intention was to shoot down the opponent's aircraft and not kill the pilot in it. In most cases a downed aircraft resulted in the death of the defeated pilot.

There is no date for the entry but it was made after he had attended the scene of an aircraft which he had shot down.

'The journey to the trenches was rather nauseating – Dead men's legs sticking through the sides with puttees and boots still on – Bits of bones and skull with hair peeled off and tons of equipment and clothing lying about. This sort of thing together with the strong stench and the dead and mangled body of the pilot, combined to upset me for a few days.'

An entry for Mannock on Wikipedia gives the following description of him: 'He also gained a reputation for ruthless hatred of German adversaries, delighting in burning them to death.'

By the time of his own death he had amassed a total of sixty-one confirmed kills as well as a further seven unconfirmed kills. He is regarded by some as the greatest

JOYCE GREEN

fighter pilot of the First World War.

Joyce Green had also been home to pilots from the Royal Naval Air Service as well as the Royal Flying Corps 39, 50 and 112 Squadrons. To add to its mystique it was also used as a Wireless Testing Centre from 1916 for the remainder of the war.

Harold and Frank Sowter Barnwell were England's answer to the world famous Wright brothers. In 1909 Harold successfully flew a biplane of their own design, and in doing so made the record books by becoming the first ever recorded instance of powered flight in Scotland. In 1912 Harold became the chief test pilot for Vickers at their factory in Surrey. He was killed on 25 August 1917 in a flying accident when he crashed in a Vickers FB26 Vampire prototype at Joyce Green Aerodrome. He is buried at St Mary's Church in Byfleet, Surrey.

Harold Barnwell.

His brother Frank, had joined the Royal Flying Corps soon after the outbreak of war in August 1914, but by the following August he had been released from his flying commitments so that he could become the chief aircraft designer in Bristol. Regrettably he was destined to die in similar circumstances at Whitstable aerodrome in 1938 whilst test flying a Barnwell BSW, an aircraft he had designed. As if that was not sad enough, Frank's three sons, Richard Anthony, John Sandes and David Usher, who were all pilots in the Royal Air Force, all perished during the Second World War.

First to be killed was 20-year-old Pilot Officer John Sandes Barnwell who died on 19 June 1940. He is buried at Scopwick Church Cemetery in Lincolnshire. During the war No. 12 Fighter Group operated out of nearby Digby Aerodrome, whose job it was to protect northern England from German aerial attacks. Those killed were usually buried at Scopwick Church. He was a holder of the King's Medal.

Flight Lieutenant Richard Anthony Barnwell, at 24, the eldest of the brothers, was killed just four months later on 29 October 1940, two days before the end of the Battle of Britain. His name is commemorated on the Air Forces Memorial at Runnymede in Surrey. The memorial contains the names of 20,456 airmen who have no known grave.

Pilot Officer David Usher Barnwell DFC, was killed on 14 October 1941. He was only 19 years of age. He is commemorated on the Malta Memorial in the Floriana area of the Island. It contains the names of 2,298 Commonwealth airmen who were killed in and around the Mediterranean and who have no known grave.

CHAPTER FIVE

Dartford through the eyes of the Press

Daily and weekly newspapers are an obvious source for historians when looking for information, although in respect of war time this was usually balanced by the restrictions about what could and couldn't be reported by the press.

In the First World War the British Government invoked the Defence of the Realm Act, more often referred to by its acronym DORA. This provided the government with extremely wide sweeping powers over the civilian population. Despite these restrictions there were still some interesting and unusual stories which made their way past the censor and on to the pages of the press. Here are some of them:

***Birmingham Daily Post* – Thursday, 6 August 1914**

ALLEGED SPY

'At Bow Street Magistrates Court, before Mr Graham Campbell, Max Bernstein Laurens (42) a British Subject, described as a Music Hall entertainer of Aide Road, Hammersmith, was charged under the Official Secrets Act 1911 with obtaining sketches, plans, documents and information which might be useful to an enemy.'

The man had been arrested by police after having visited the offices of the Admiralty in London. When later charged Laurens replied: *'I do not understand this at all; I went to the Admiralty to offer my services and they have had me arrested. I have done service for them before, as you can prove if you make enquiries at the Colonial Office.'*

He had previously worked at Vickers, Sons and Maxim at their Dartford Cartridge Works. The man was remanded in custody and what ultimately happened to him isn't known.

Newcastle Journal, **Thursday, 5 November 1914**

ALLEGED ATTEMPTED MURDER OF A SOLDIER

'At Grays, Essex yesterday, Laura Pearson, a 19-year-old girl residing at Dartford was charged with the attempted murder of a soldier.

It was stated that the accused had been walking out with Private Horace Caller of the South-West Kent Regiment, and on Tuesday visited him at Purfleet Camp, Essex. There was some difference between them, and when she asked him to go for a walk with her, he refused. She asked him to kiss her, which he did, and it is alleged while doing so the girl took a razor from her muff and inflicted a wound to his throat. He was treated at the Military hospital. The girl was remanded.'

Private 980 Horace Caller was a member of the Transport Section, 'D' Company, 6th Battalion, Queen's Own (Royal West Kent) Regiment, which was part of the British Expeditionary Force's 12th Division. He enlisted in the army on 1 September 1914 at Maidstone, Kent. He survived the war, being stabbed in the throat was the worst injury he sustained during his service. He was demobbed at Purfleet on 21 January 1919 and was awarded the British War Medal, the Victory Medal as well as the 1915 Star, having first arrived in France on 1 June 1915.

He did eventually get married, but not to Laura Pearson. On Christmas Eve 1916, he married Gertrude Downer at Beckenham in Kent. He died in March 1974 in Dartford, aged 83.

All that is known of Laura Pearson is from what is recorded on the 1911 Census, which shows that she lived at 'Clevis', New Barn, Longfield, Kent, where she was a servant for a Mr Henry Cory and his one-year-old son, Kenneth Cory.

Kent & Sussex Courier – **Friday, 2 April 1915**

CITY OF LONDON ASYLUM

'Male attendants wanted, wages £32 10s rising to £47 10s in ten years, and by long service and promotion to £55 10s (Subject to deductions under the Asylum Officers Superannuation Act 1909), with board, lodging, washing and after probation, uniform; no one eligible for enlistment in the Army or Navy need apply.'

The need for the last sentence threw up an interesting scenario; it was almost as if there was a belief by those who governed the asylum that men would apply for the position in the hope that it would preclude them from having to serve in the military.

The above advert appeared in the newspaper's Situations Vacant column. It apparently didn't get any response from prospective job seekers as the same advert was back in the newspaper the following week.

A general theme which cropped up on a regular basis throughout the newspaper articles was the rise in costs of beef, coal and wages.

Essex Newsman – **Saturday 19 June 1915**

WAR NEWS

'Lieutenant A. Quick, 6th Essex Regiment of Clacton, recently serving at Dartford, has been appointed Adjutant at the Orchard Hospital, Dartford, where 1,200 convalescent soldiers are to be accommodated.'

Manchester Courier and Lancashire General Advertiser – **Wednesday, 28 July 1915**

'Notice was given in last night's London Gazette that the Central Control Board for Liquor Traffic, have issued an order applying the liquor control regulations to the area of the Dartford district in the County of Kent.'

Drunkenness was becoming a big problem across the country, more so because it was starting to have an effect on industries directly concerned with the war effort. When people failed to turn up to work because they were hung over it had a marked impact on production targets.

The same article also appeared in the *Birmingham Daily Post* (28 July 1915), and the *Aberdeen Evening Express* (16 July 1915).

Manchester Evening News – **Saturday, 28 August 1915**

AIRMAN HERO'S FUNERAL

'Captain Gilbert William Richard Maplebeck DSO, the first airman to carry out reconnaissances and drop bombs over the German lines, was buried with full military honours at Streatham Cemetery today.

The deceased officer, after serving with distinction for more than six months abroad, winning the DSO for his bravery, was killed while trying a new machine at Dartford. Many of the deceased's fellow officers from the King's (Liverpool) Regiment and the Flying Corps attended, including General Sir David Henderson.'

There is an interesting story attached to Gilbert. To start with the 1911 Census shows him living with his mother, Sarah, his younger brother Godfrey, age three, along with two servants, at Olive Vale, Wavertree, Nook, Liverpool. He was already in the military, shown as being a second lieutenant in the King's (Liverpool) Regiment at the age of 18. The census records his middle names as William Roger and not William Richard. The spelling of his surname was with two Ps and not one. Perhaps his father, William, had separated from his mother, as the 1911 Census showed him as living in Barnston, Doncaster with his sister and her nine-year-old son.

Gilbert was born in Liverpool on 26 August 1892. Whilst still in the King's (Liverpool) Regiment he acquired his flying certificate on 7 January 1913 after taking a course at the Deperdussin Flying School at Hendon. By September 1914 he was in France as part of No. 4 Squadron.

On 29 September 1914 he was flying over the British retreat at Mons when he became embroiled in a duel with German aircraft at 6,000 feet. In the ensuing melée he was shot but managed to reach the British lines where he landed his aircraft and then passed out from his wounds. He then spent three months in hospital recovering from his injuries.

With the distinction of having been the first British pilot to carry out a reconnaissance flight over enemy lines, as well as being the first to drop bombs on German ground troops, 'tucked under his belt' he then went on to become the first pilot involved in a night bombing raid when, along with two colleagues, he set off to bomb the French city of Lille. Unfortunately luck was not to be on his side. He was shot down by German aircraft but still managed to land safely. Rather than risk letting his aircraft fall into enemy hands he set fire to it and made good his escape; and then hid in a wood for three days with only chocolate to sustain him.

Able to speak fluent French and with the help of some local people, including the Mayor of Lille, Monsieur Camille Eugene Jacquet, Mapplebeck dressed as a French peasant and made his way on foot to the Dutch border. Once in Holland he made his way back to England where he arrived on 4 April 1915. When the Germans eventually discovered Mapplebeck had been assisted to escape Jacquet and three others were executed.

Mapplebeck returned briefly to the Western Front before going back to England in June 1915 having been transferred to No 2 Reserve Aeroplane Squadron stationed at Joyce Green Aerodrome, near Dartford.

On the evening of Tuesday, 24 August 1915, just three days before his twenty-third birthday and already a holder of the Distinguished Service Order, he was flying a French Morane-Saulnier Type N aircraft when it crashed at Joyce Green Aerodrome, killing him instantly. He was buried at Streatham Cemetery in London. The cortège was accompanied on the journey from Dartford to Streatham by a guard of honour from the Royal Flying Corps. The mourners included his brother Second Lieutenant T.G. Mapplebeck, also of the King's (Liverpool) Regiment. He was wounded at the Battle of Neuve Chappelle in France and after recovering from his wounds, he too joined the Royal Flying Corps.

Gilbert's death even provoked Royal comment. A letter was given to his mother, Sarah, by Lord Stamfordham which read:

'Dear Madam, I am commanded by the King to convey to you the

assurance of His Majesty's true sympathy with you in the cruel loss which you have sustained in the death of your son through an accident when flying a new machine at Dartford.

His Majesty knows what gallant and distinguished services he has rendered during the war, and deeply regrets that a young life of such promise should have been thus cut short.'

In his will Gilbert left his estate, which was valued at £175 15s 9d, to his father, William.

Lichfield Mercury – **Friday, 29 October 1915**

HEAVY DAMAGE BY FIRE AT DARTFORD

'Early on Monday morning a destructive fire broke out at Lower Hythe Street, Dartford, doing considerable damage to the premises of Messr's R.N.H. Strickland, corn merchants. The fire spread with great rapidity owing to the wind, and the following property was severely damaged: a building used as a grain store completely burned to the ground; the premises of the Dartford Wharfage Company. Victoria Wharf; two wood pulp stacks, one of about 1500 tons, and the other of about 500 tons, and about 600 tons of timber: the dumb barge, Cawnpore, laden with timber; the sailing barge Prompt, also laden with timber.

The damage is estimated at £10,000. Some very large works nearby were also threatened, and were only saved by the hard work of a number of brigades.'

Dundee Courier – **Friday, 24 December 1915**

A GERMAN LEPER

'Mr Tennant, replying to Mr Butler Lloyd, said that special accommodation had been prepared for the German prisoner who was in an advanced condition of leprosy at a hospital at Dartford.'

The same story also appeared in other national and local daily and weekly publications. Before being moved to Dartford the German prisoner had been held for many months at Handforth Barracks near Manchester immediately next to the camp's guardroom.

Birmingham Daily Post – **Wednesday, 29 December 1915**

ALLEGATIONS AGAINST A SOLDIER

'Private Jesse Williamson was remanded at Dartford yesterday, charged with entering a house in Dartford Road, Westhill, on Christmas morning and stealing £5 and a revolver. It was further alleged that Williamson shot at Mr Bates, the householder, who received such severe injuries that he had to be removed to hospital. Williamson, who was arrested at Wood Green, had been absent from his Regiment for some weeks.'

Grantham Journal – **Saturday, 11 March 1916**

A MILITARY WEDDING

'An interesting wedding took place at Dartford on Wednesday, the 8th inst., between Miss W.A. Garwood, elder daughter of the late Mr W.E. Garwood, of Thurlby, and Sergeant E.W. Bloomfield, Army Service Corps. The marriage was celebrated in the Dartford Wesleyan Chapel by the Rev W.H. Phipps BA. The bride, who was attired in a travelling costume of navy-blue trimmed with military braids, was given away by her brother-in-law, Mr W.T. Robinson. A detachment of the Mechanical Transport staff attended from the Grove Park Barracks as a guard of honour, Sergeant J. Noble officiated as best man. The happy couple departed by the 10am train from Dartford, en-route for Torquay, where the honeymoon is being spent.'

Nottingham Evening Post – **Monday, 3 April 1916**

DEATH OF CANON P.E. SMITH

'The death has taken place of Canon Percy Edward Smith, Vicar of Dartford. Graduating at Trinity College, Dublin, in 1889, he proceeded to MA, in 1888. After holding a curacy at Coolkenno, Co. Wicklow, Canon Smith was appointed curate of Lenton, and he held that position from 1881 to 1886. He was then offered the living, and this he accepted remaining until 1893. During his vicariate he was instrumental in restoring the Oriory Church. In

the last mentioned year he was appointed Vicar of Dartford, and he was made Hon. Canon of Rochester in 1909.'

Tamworth Herald – Saturday 27 May 1916

SERGEANT'S DEATH

'The death has occurred at Dartford War Hospital, of Sergeant Archibald James Grubb, of the Royal Defence Corps, Dartmouth. Sergeant Grubb formerly lived at Middleton, and was son-in-law of Mrs Britt, of 82 Bolebridge Street, Tamworth. He had been practically all his life in the Army. As a lad he enlisted as a bugler in the 4th Norfolks; later he joined the Scots Guards, and afterwards transferred to the West Kents. He was organist and choirmaster at Codlinge Church, near Rochester.'

Birmingham Daily Post – Friday, 9 June 1916

LOSS ON FEEDING THE TROOPS

'In his bankruptcy examination at Rochester, a Dartford licensed victualler said he lost over £1,500 on a contract for feeding the troops. He provided three meals daily, and the War Office reduced the price from 2s to 1s 7d per soldier per day.

Newcastle Journal – Friday, 29 September 1916

WOMEN AS ARMY COOKS

The Director of the Military Cookery Section of the Women's Legion, E. Londonderry, wrote the following letter to the *Newcastle Journal* on the topic of Women as Army Cooks.

'Sir – In view of the urgent and constant need of women as Army cooks, I am writing to ask you if you would kindly insert the following in your paper at your very earliest convenience.

A school of cookery has been started at Dartford Convalescent Camp for training women for the military cookery section of the Women's Legion. The course of instruction lasts from three to four weeks and there are vacancies for 30 pupils in each course. The instruction comprises camp cooking as well as the kitchen routine. The women in training must be between the ages of 18 and 35.

Free rations and quarters will be provided at the camp, but the women receive no pay during their term of instruction, but if satisfactory at the completion of their training they are drafted on wherever required, and receive pay at the rate of £20 per annum, rations and accommodation, etc. The women are required before entering the course to sign an agreement to the effect that they will serve on after their training for 12 months or the duration of the war.

In making the most urgent appeal for this most vital work in connection with the Army, it is hoped that many women would serve as camp cooks, but who have refrained from coming forward on account of not having sufficient knowledge, will volunteer for this work and join these classes.

The military cookery section of the Women's Legion has already supplied over 1200 women as cooks and waitresses in the convalescent camps, command depots, training camps, officers, and non-commissioned officers' messes in all parts of England, thus releasing men for active service.'

Dartford Camp 1st Woolwich G Corps Cooks.

Although most in the above photograph are men, notice the woman in the middle of the background of the photograph.

Aberdeen Journal – **Tuesday, 6 February 1917**

ESCAPED GERMAN RECAPTURED

'The German, Otto Wudtko, who was reported to have escaped from an escort which was taking a party of prisoners from Knockaloo to the war hospital at Dartford, has been recaptured.'

Wudtko had escaped on 1 February after having left the Knockoloo prisoner of war camp on the Isle of Man, en route to Dartford and had been on the run for three days before his recapture.

Birmingham Gazette – **Thursday, 29 March 1917**

BEER IS 1s A PINT

'A Rochester correspondent learns that the brewers of Kent have fixed their prices, so that on Monday next mild beer will be 7d and bitter 1s a pint in the districts of Chatham, Gravesend and Dartford, and 5d and 8d a pint respectively in other parts of Kent.'

Evening Telegraph – **Friday, 16 March 1917**

REMARKABLE STORY IN SEPARATION SUIT

'It is sometimes suggested that the cruelty on which the Divorce Court grants decrees to unhappy wives is more a matter of imagination than reality. No such objection could be made against a case established before the President today. Mrs Lucy Annie Nanley, wife of Arthur Douglas Nanley, licensee of the Smith's Arms, Dartford, had, according to the evidence given, an extraordinary list of acts of violence to lay to her husband's charge. He did not defend the petition, which was judicial separation.

The following is the list, the events happening at Dartford and Bexhill-on-Sea.

(1). Mr Nanley came upon his wife suddenly as she was walking in a public garden, and thrashed her across the back with a cane.

(2). When she was driving with him she complained of his beating the horse. He struck her in the face with his hat.

(3). He struck her with his fist in the mouth so that she could not eat for three weeks.

(4). He knocked her down on some slippery linoleum, and when she asked him to help her to get up, kicked her.

(5). She was late when they were about to go for a drive. As she was getting in to the trap he snatched her hat off and threw it in to the yard.

(6). They were staying at Weymouth, and were walking on the beach. She did not agree with on a subject they were discussing, and he hit her with his walking stick.

(7). He struck her on the nose as she was sitting in an armchair.

(8). They were having tea in the kitchen. She took her cup and saucer to go with it to the drawing room. As he walked out he kicked the cup and saucer out of her hand.

On another occasion she escaped from him into the servant's bedroom, barricaded the door with the bed. He broke in with a crowbar. She got out of the window on to the sill, and then fell to the ground, breaking both her thighs.

The President thought the case for cruelty fully made out and granted the decree asked for.'

Mrs Nanley must have been very strong, determined and brave as life; for a woman in 1917 was very different from today. The Suffragettes and the women's movement in general, were still in their relative infancy. Generally women were seen as second-class citizens whose job it was to get married, have children and stay at home and look after their husbands and children. When married they were then seen as their husband's property.

It was after the war in 1918 that women were first given the right to vote as a result of the Representation of the People Act 1918, but even then it was only for women over 30 years of age who owned a property. The same Act provided for all men over the age of 21 with the right to vote, regardless of class or wealth. Men in the armed forces were allowed to vote from the age of 19. It would be a further ten years before that was lowered to the age of 21 with the introduction of the Equal Franchise Act 1928.

***Essex Newsman* – Saturday, 21 April 1917**

A RED CROSS WEDDING

'The wedding of Mr Charles E.L. Newitt, son of Col E.J. Newitt, Thorpe Bay, with Miss Daisy M. Choppen, daughter of Mr W.H. Choppen, of Thundersley, took place at Darenth Parish Church, Kent. The bride, who has been attached to the VAD at the War Hospital, Dartford, was married in the uniform of the British Red Cross Society. Mr Lionel Flowers, of Romford, was best man. After the ceremony the bride and bridegroom passed under an archway of wooden spoons tied with the national colours, and a reception was held at the Hospital. The bridegroom is Commandant of the Men's VAD (Essex 51).'

***Coventry Evening Telegraph* – Saturday, 2 June 1917**

FOOD OFFENCE FINES

'Manageress at Messrs. Vickers hostel for munition workers, Margaret Dunk, was at Dartford on Friday, fined £2 for a breach of the food restriction orders, it being stated that slices of bread and a piece of meat were found in a dustbin. Notice of appeal was given.'

***Birmingham Gazette* – Wednesday, 13 June 1917**

STRUGGLE IN TRAIN

'A story of a desperate struggle in a railway carriage was told at Dartford when Bernard Cook, of Milton Court Road, New Cross, appeared on remand charged with doing grievous bodily harm to Miss Edith May, a clerk employed at the Park Hospital, Lewisham.

Miss May said she lived at Well Meadow Road, Lewisham. On 5 June she was travelling from Dartford to Hither Green. Just before the train started the prisoner got in and sat opposite to her. She noticed him undoing his coat and putting his hand underneath, but took no notice. The next thing she remembered *was the prisoner striking her on the jaw with some heavy instrument.*

He struck her several blows on the head. She turned to reach the communications cord, but the prisoner knocked her down on the floor. She screamed, and the prisoner tried to put his hand over her mouth. She got to the window and shouted "Murder!"

Eventually the train stopped and she saw a man named Hurst, of the RNAS come to the carriage with the guard and another man. She had been to the bank at Dartford and had over £50 in a small bag.

Ernest Richard Hurst, RNAS, said that after the train left Crayford he heard screams from one of the compartments. He got out while the train was in motion and walked along the footboard to the compartment occupied by prisoner. When he looked in he saw Miss May on the floor smothered in blood, and the prisoner standing over in the attitude of striking. He appeared to have an iron bar in his hand. Witness then went back to his own carriage and pulled the communication cord. The prisoner at once jumped out of the train on to the line from the opposite side.

Dr Walker, of Bexley, said when he examined Miss May he found her covered in blood and suffering from several serious cuts. He thought the wounds were caused by some blunt instrument, as they were too jagged to have been done by a knife. Considerable force must have been used.

Inspector Muir proved the arrest of prisoner. There was blood on his collar, waistcoat and shirt.

The Prisoner, who reserved his defence, was committed for trial at the next assizes.'

Western Times – Wednesday, 11 July 1917

RFC MAN'S DEATH IN THE AIR RAID

'An inquest at Dartford yesterday, on Second Lieutenant Wilfred Graham Salmon, RFC, killed in Saturday's air raid, evidence showed that his machine fell spinning sideways. Deceased had a wound in the head probably caused by a bullet, and his petrol punctured by a bullet. A verdict of "death from fractured skull

received by a fall, and from wounds received in combat with German aeroplanes" was returned.'

Derby Daily Telegraph – Friday, 20 July 1917

SMOKING IN MUNITONS FACTORY – INSPECTOR'S BAD EXAMPLE

'At Dartford Police Court today, Edward Digby, an Inspector at Messrs. Vickers Ltd, whose duty it was to enforce regulations prohibiting smoking in the factory, was fined £20 for smoking a cigarette in the factory. The defendant said he did not realise that he had the cigarette in his mouth. He admitted the danger.'

It can only be assumed that the entire court fell in to a fit of laughter on hearing Mr Digby's words of explanation!

Manchester Evening News – Friday, 27 July 1917

SOUVENIRS TAKEN FROM AIRMAN'S BODY

'At Dartford, Kent five women and four men were fined £1 each for being in possession of public property. The case was a sequel to an air raid on London of July 7, when Lieutenant Salmon, who fought the raiders, crashed to the ground. It was stated that a number of parts of the machine had been carried away, and that some of the personal belongings of the dead officer had also been removed. The gloves, safety belt, and goggles worn by Lieutenant Salmon had been recovered by the Police. They must have been taken off the dead body.'

In court the defendants all claimed that they 'were acting innocently' when they removed parts of the aircraft and personal items form Lieutenant Salmon's body; quite how each of them arrived at that deduction is unclear.

Evening Telegraph – Tuesday, 7 August 1917

MARATHON RECORD

'C. Giles of the 1st Cavalry Reserve, put up a fine performance yesterday at Vickers Dartford sports, winning the 15 mile open

marathon in 1 hour 22 and a half minutes, believed to be a record.'

This equates to a speed of five and a half minute miles. As the marathon distance is now 26.2 miles, if C. Giles could have sustained the same speed, he would have finished what now constitutes the marathon distance in 2 hours 24 minutes and 10 seconds. The current distance was first run at the 1908 Olympics on 24 July, but didn't become the standard distance for the marathon until 1921. The race was won by American Johnny Hayes, in what was then a new Olympic time of 2 hours 55 minutes and 18 seconds, making Giles's time more than respectable.

Taunton Courier & Western Advertiser – Wednesday 15 August 1917

'Early on Tuesday morning the train sheds at Dartford and the whole of the cars in the service were destroyed by fire. It is asserted that cries were heard from the burning building, but the night man, who left at midnight, states that the building was empty, all lights out, and the electric current turned off. London cars have been applied for.'

Evening Telegraph – Friday, 17 August 1917

SMOKED IN EXPLOSIVES FACTORY

'At Dartford today, Thomas Dann was fined £5 for smoking in an explosives factory. Defendant had been employed by the firm for twenty years. His excuse was that he had a very bad toothache, and was trying to cure it.'

Western Times – Tuesday, 28 August 1917

DARTFORD AIR FATALITY

'The inquest was held at Dartford yesterday on Richard Harold Barnwell, an accomplished aviator, who was killed whilst flying at a Kentish aerodrome on Saturday. Mr Harold Savage, the manager at Messrs. Vickers Ltd, said the deceased was their chief pilot and tester. He had not been in good health recently, but he had been up previously on the day of his death. Witness formed

the opinion that Mr Barnwell was taken ill during the flight and lost control of the machine. A verdict of "death by misadventure" was returned.

It was interesting to note that the article didn't identify the actual location Barnwell had been flying from, which was Joyce Green Aerodrome, on the outskirts of Dartford, most probably because of reporting restrictions brought in as part of the Defence of the Realm Act. That credit was given to Mr Savage's comments about what he believed was the reason behind why Barnwell crashed, was surprising, especially as it could just as easily have been down to mechanical failure of the aircraft.

Evening Telegraph *– **Tuesday, 25 September 1917***

AIRMAN'S DIVE TO EARTH

'Lieutenant Munn, of the Royal Flying Corps, was killed at Dartford yesterday afternoon through his aeroplane nose dipping and crashing to earth. The observer, who jumped from the aeroplane, was seriously injured.'

Aberdeen Journal *– **Tuesday, 25 September 1917***

MUNITIONER AND INCOME TAX

'S.G. Richards, a 20-year-old munition worker, employed by Messrs Vickers, who was said to have earned £18 in one week, was sent to prison for 28 days at Dartford last week for the non-payment of £8 19s 6d income tax.

It was stated that for the last four weeks he had earned £3 8s 1d, £6 7s 6d, £9 9s 1d, and £6 18s 7d, and during the last two years he had earned on an average £12 a week.'

Birmingham Post *– **Tuesday, 6 November 1917***

FATAL FALL ON TO A BRIDGE

'An aeroplane fell on to a barge which was sailing down the Thames at Dartford. The aeroplane pilot, an RFC Captain was instantly killed, and his observer was seriously injured.'

Aberdeen Journal – **Thursday, 8 November 1917**

ALLEGED OFFENCE AGAINST ALIENS ORDER

'At Dartford yesterday, George Papamkaiav, described as a Greek, was charged with aiding and abetting Alias Tirelis to commit an offence against the Aliens Order. Tirelis is one of six aliens undergoing a month's imprisonment and recommended for deportation for giving false particulars as to their nationality.

Tirelis, in evidence, stated that he went to the accused, who was employed at the British Legation in Athens, and who, he said, supplied him with a certificate stating that he was born in Cyprus, and therefore was a British subject. As a matter of fact, he was born in Smyrna.

The Police stated that accused was missed while at work in a munition factory in January, and was arrested a few days ago in Aberdeen.

The accused denied all knowledge of the man Tirelis and others except that he saw them on a boat, and also denied having handed over any certificates or taken any money. He fought with the British at the Dardanelles and was wounded in the Royalist attack on the Legation in Athens.

The magistrates discharged the accused.'

Kent & Sussex Courier – **Friday, 23 November 1917**

HILDENBOROUGH

'Mr Joseph Martin, of Bourne Place Cottages, Hildenborough, has received news that another of his sons, Sergeant Joseph Martin, RGA, was killed in action on November 1st by the bursting of a shell. He was 30 years of age, and previous to the war had served nine years with the Colours, five years in India. He came out on the Reserve in March 1914 and joined the Kent Constabulary, being stationed at Dartford. He was called up at the outbreak of the war.'

Joseph had two brothers, George and Frederick. The latter was a bombardier, also in the Royal Garrison Artillery when he was killed in action on the Western Front on 27 July 1917. He was 34 years of age.

Manchester Evening News – **Saturday, 15 December 1917**

A TRAGEDY OF WAR PROFITS

'A verdict of suicide during insanity was returned at a Dartford inquest, today, on a master stevedore, named William Bates, a large employer of labour, whose body was recovered from Dartford Creek. It was stated that on Wednesday morning the deceased received a claim from excess profits amounting to nearly £6,000, and also a large claim for the income tax, neither of which he had paid since the outbreak of the war. Bates was greatly troubled, and expressed his intention of committing suicide as he could not stick it.'

Aberdeen Evening Express – **Wednesday, 23 January 1918**

FIRED BY BOYS

'At Dartford (Kent) Police Court yesterday three boys, Ernest Cecil Adams (14), Fred George Blogg (15), and Harold Wesley Gurr (14), were charged with setting fire to the old training ship Warspite, which was destroyed by fire during Sunday night in the Thames off Greenhithe. The three defendants were members of the Warspite's crew.

According to Police evidence, Gurr who, with the other two, was arrested on HMS Worcester, where they were taken after the fire, stated that he was invited in to the hold by the other two boys, where he found a heap of pieces of wood and canvas and other rubbish, to which Blogg set fire.

Adams corroborated this statement, and Blogg who refused to say anything on that occasion, made a statement yesterday morning admitting that he set fire to the ship. He said that arrangements had been made to do it before the Christmas leave.

Prisoners were remanded until Friday.'

Birmingham Daily Mail – **Wednesday, 30 January 1918**

WARSPITE AFFAIR – HALF THE BOYS SAID TO BE IMPLICATED

'When the three Warspite boys were brought before the Dartford

Magistrates yesterday charged with setting fire to the training ship Warspite on January 20 the prosecuting council stated that the vessel was insured for £10,000, and everything had been consumed by the fire.

Captain A.K. Hill, superintendent of the ship, said there were 240 boys on board, and enough stores for three months. While acknowledging that flogging was one of the punishments on board, he denied any knowledge of a revolt among the boys, or of flogging being resorted to more than once or twice weekly.

Herbert Offord, one of the Warspite boys, said half the ship agreed that the prisoners should set fire to it.

The three boys were committed for trial, defence being reserved.'

Derby Daily Telegraph – Friday, 1 March 1918

KING AND QUEEN VISIT DARTFORD COLLEGE

'The King and Queen today visited the college at Dartford where young ladies are taught physical exercise to qualify them as instructresses for physical training in the elementary schools of the country. Their Majesties visited the laboratory; saw the children under treatment for spinal complaints (the college is used also as a kind of hospital), and a variety of physical exercises. At the conclusion of the visit all the students assembled at the exit and cheered their Majesties as they drove away.'

Birmingham Daily Post – Saturday, 6 March 1918

MUNITION WORKERS AND THEIR HOUSES

'An important decision was given by Dartford Magistrates yesterday in a case in which an ejectment order was sought. It was contended for the defence that by an order issued by the Minister of Munitions, protection was given to munition workers against eviction from their houses without the authority of the Department. The order came into force on March 5, and the notice to leave in this case was given on March 7. The daughter of the tenant had been engaged on munition work, but was at present at

home looking after her mother, who was ill. She proposed however, to return to work as soon as her mother had recovered. It was contended for the owner of the house that the daughter had ceased to be a munition worker, and that the order did not apply in consequence, but the Chairman said the Bench ruled otherwise, and therefore they would not make an order for eviction.'

Aberdeen Evening Express – Thursday, 9 May 1918

FLYING FATALITY OVER TOWN

'Two pilots and an observer were killed in a collision between two aeroplanes which occurred over Dartford on Tuesday night. The victims were Captain Bertram James, Lieutenant Gordon Nash and Lieutenant James Gordon Ward.

The accident was witnessed by a large number of people, the machines having been performing revolutions over the town for some time. Shortly before eight o'clock the aeroplanes came into collision, and one was seen to nose dive to the ground.

Captain James had acted as an instructor at an aerodrome for about two months. Lieut. Nash's home is not far from the scene of the accident.'

Evening Telegraph – Friday, 10 May 1918

ALLEGED EXTENSIVE THEFTS OF GOODS IN TRANSIT

'At Dartford today a guard and shunter employed by the South Eastern and Chatham Railway, together with the guard's wife, were remanded in connection with alleged extensive thefts of goods in transit.

It was stated the shunter was seen carrying parcels along the railway, and was found to have fifteen packets of confectionary, while in the guards house were found bottles of wine and spirits hidden in the garden, and cases of butter and packets of cocoa and tea in various parts of the house.'

Western Daily Press – Tuesday, 28 May 1918

'A young woman named Nancy Hilda Martin was remanded at Dartford Police Court yesterday charged with the attempted

murder of John Julius Chambers, a prominent Kent agriculturist, by stabbing him in the back with a knife.'

Lancashire Evening Post – Tuesday, 4 June 1918

COLLISION 2000 FEET UP

'An inquest was held at Dartford yesterday, concerning the deaths of Lieutenant Frank Leslie Shield and Lieutenant John Percival Van Ryneveld, two flying officers, whose machines collided in the air on Sunday. Lieutenant Herbert Griffiths said the officers were fully experienced pilots. At the time of the accident they were about 2,000 feet up. The back part of one machine collided with the centre of the other, and both came down to earth. The probable cause was that the sun was in the eyes of one of the pilots, as officers have been forbidden fighting practice without arrangement previously made. Verdict of death from misadventure.'

Evening Telegraph – Tuesday, 2 July 1918

MAN WHO HAD NEVER BEEN IN THE ARMY WORE DECORATIONS TO AVOID BEING CALLED A SHIRKER

'Sidney Herbert Simms (27), of Gravesend, was sentenced to four months imprisonment at Dartford today for posing as a discharged soldier by wearing the Mons ribbon, two wound stripes, and three chevrons. He had never served in the Army.

He pleaded he wore the decorations to avoid being called a shirker.'

Hull Daily Mail – Monday, 19 August 1918

AN AUSTRALIAN ARMY

'In presenting the prizes at sports for the patients of the Dartford Military Hospital on Saturday, Mr Hughes, Premier of Australia, said in the great battles of the past few days no Army of the Allies had achieved greater success than the Australians. The maximum advance made in the last attack was 13 miles.

"This attack," he said, "Will always be remembered as the first

great battle in which all the Australian troops fought together as one Army under an Australian General and with all Australian officers. We had our own magnificent infantry, artillery, and mounted men, our own air force, engineers, transport, medical services and in fact, all the units which go to make up a great Army.

Australia is also strongly represented in the Navy . . . and thousands of her men are now helping to increase the supply of munitions in the factories of Great Britain."'

Western Daily Press – **Friday, 18 October 1918**

'The King, Queen, and Princess Mary yesterday afternoon paid a visit to an American base hospital at Dartford. The Royal party, who had a splendid reception, made a tour of the wards, and strolled through the grounds, chatting with the patients.'

CHAPTER SIX

Military Service Tribunals

During the first eighteen months of the First World War more than three million men came forward to volunteer to serve in the British military. Three factors then came in to play to change this initial, almost blind, enthusiasm. Firstly, the war had already lasted much longer than anyone had ever expected. Secondly, the numbers of men who had either been wounded or killed were astronomically high. By December 1914 Britain had already suffered almost 99,000 casualties – including those who had been killed, wounded, were missing in action or who had been taken prisoner. Thirdly, the true horror of the war was there for all to see. Too many families had already been directly affected by the war, laying bare the myth that it would all be over by Christmas after giving the Hun a bloody nose.

To deal with the need for more men to go and fight, the British Government decided to bring in compulsory conscription in the shape of the Military Service Act 1916, which was first used on 2 March 1916. It decreed that all single men aged between 18 and 41, were liable to be called up for military service, the only exceptions being either men who were religious ministers or widowed men with children to support. Within less than three months the authorities realised they still didn't have sufficient manpower for the armed forces, so on 25 May 1916, the criteria for eligibility was changed to include married men. As the war raged on, and with more and more men being either killed or wounded, the age limit was eventually raised to 51, regardless of a man's personal circumstances.

With the need to bring in compulsory conscription, so was there a need to deal with those who refused to answer the call to serve, no matter what their reason. This was done in the shape of Military Service Tribunals, which would ultimately determine if a man's request not to be called up would be listened to sufficiently to prevent him from having to serve in the military.

Each local council put in place their own Military Service Tribunal to hear individual applications for exemption from compulsory conscription into the British Army. Across the county there were just over 2,000 local tribunals as well as a further 83 county ones which dealt solely with appeals. On top of this was a tribunal which sat at Westminster in London that considered particularly difficult cases which had been forwarded to them by an Appeals Tribunal. Their decision was final.

Men who had been called up for military service initially had the right to apply to their local Military Tribunal for a certificate of exemption. If they lost their case they could then appeal this decision to the County appeal tribunal. Within the first four months of compulsory conscription, 748,587 men had made applications to their local tribunals giving a plethora of reasons as to why they should be exempt from being called up. During the same period a similar number of men had joined the British Army.

Three main forms were used in this process; firstly there was the form that was used to make the initial application which was the R-41 form or the 'Application as to Exemption'. When the application had been dealt with by the tribunal, an R.57 form, or the 'Notice of Decision' would be issued to the applicant informing them of the outcome of their case. If this was in the negative and the applicant wished to appeal the tribunal's decision, they had to complete an R-43 form, or the 'Notice of Appeal'. The first two of these forms was a buff colour whilst the latter was salmon pink.

The grounds on which a man could apply for an exemption certificate came under any one of three different headings. He could seek an absolute exemption, which is self-explanatory, or he could apply for a conditional or temporary exemption. He had seven grounds on which he could make an appeal, these were as follows:

- That it is expedient in the national interests that the man should, instead of being employed in military service, be engaged in other work in which he is habitually engaged.
- That it is expedient in the national interests that the man should, instead of being employed in military service, be engaged in other work in which he wishes to be engaged.
- If he is being educated or trained for any work, on the ground that it is expedient in the national interests that, instead of being employed in military service, he should continue to be educated or trained.
- That serious hardship would endure if the man were called up for army service, owing to his exceptional financial or business obligations or domestic position.
- On the ground of ill health or infirmity.
- On the ground of a conscientious objection to the undertaking of combative service.
- That the principle and usual occupation of the man is one of those included in the list of occupations certified by government departments for exemption.

The exact number of men who sat before such tribunals is not known, but in the two and a half years of their existence, thousands of men did sit before them to argue their case and hope that their prayers would be answered.

Three years after the end of the First World War in 1921 the Ministry of Health Department issued a directive to all Local Government Boards advising them that paperwork and documentation appertaining to Military Service Tribunals should be destroyed. Why or how this decision was arrived at is not clear, but it is one which has certainly caused much debate amongst historians over the years.

There is no doubt that some of these tribunals would have dealt with very sensitive and personal issues, whilst others will, even today, still be a cause of deep embarrassment for the families of those concerned. There were some who saw the tribunals as nothing more than a 'Cowards Charter' and an official way of avoiding the requirement to enlist in the Army, Navy or Air Force.

Most local authorities did as they were told and destroyed the records which they held for Military Service Tribunals; thankfully not all authorities complied with this instruction, which ensured that future generations would be well informed about the intimate workings of these tribunals. Most of these records survive today in county archives and museums, and in the local newspapers which reported their proceedings.

Some people found it hard to take knowing that they had lost a loved one during the war only to hear that somewhere else, a perfectly fit, healthy young man had managed to avoid going off to fight for their king and country.

On Friday, 16 June 1916 the following article appeared in the *Kent & Sussex Courier* on the subject of Military Service Tribunals.

> *'The wriggling of the dodger, who generally is a conscientious objector, is likely to be cut short by a ruling which was given by His Honour Judge Parry at the West Kent Appeal Tribunal on Monday. New regulations were to hand, and Colonel Bathurst, one of the official representatives of the Board of Agriculture, asked for rulings upon three questions under them: (1) As regards the new regulations, are they retrospective, and if so, to what extent as regards appeals from Local Tribunals to Appeal Tribunals. (2) Has the Local Tribunal the right to refuse leave to appeal to the Appeal Tribunal and (3) What is the position of a man who has already been granted postponement by the Appeal Tribunal if he wishes further postponement? To whom must he apply?*
>
> *Judge Parry answered question one by stating that in every case dealt with by the Appeal Tribunal appeals must come to that Tribunal, while as to question three, the answer was implied in the answer to question one. Mr Prossier, the Clerk to the Tribunal also held this view, but as to question two, both he and Judge Parry expressed the opinion that a lot of consideration was required, and they therefore withheld giving any ruling upon it upon that occasion. The fact seems to remain, however, that the dodging backwards and forwards between the Local and the Appeal Tribunals which has been systematically carried on in some cases has received its finishing touch under the new regulations.'*

Local newspapers often carried reports of tribunals which had been convened to hear the objections of men who felt, for whatever reason, that they were unable to serve in the armed forces. Some objected to fighting on religious or moral grounds, others considered that their occupations were more important to the country than compulsory military service. A report of a one such tribunal hearing appeared in the *Dartford Reporter* in 1917.

It was about a man by the name of Harry Holloway, who lived in Dartford. His reason for applying for a certificate of exemption was because for him to assist in a war in any way would violate his personal feelings. He clarified the point that his reticence to fight was not based on any particularly held religious beliefs. He saw himself as being just as religious as the next man without being a particularly religious individual.

When asked by the tribunal if he was a member of any religious body, he replied that he was not, nor had he been tutored by anybody who offered to help conscientious objectors.

He was further asked if he could provide any evidence to prove that he had held these same strong beliefs before the war had started. He replied that he did not know that any people could have their views tabulated in such a way and to take part in the war would violate all of his ideals and principles, and that he did not wish to aid either side in prosecuting the war.

He said that he had for years belonged to a socialist organisation and was prepared to suffer death or any worse punishment in default of serving in the British military. When asked if he had denied himself either food or clothing that had been brought into the country by the gallantry of sailors, many of whom who had lost their lives, he admitted that he had not.

His application for a certificate of exemption was refused.

To try and find out some more about Harry I checked the 1911 Census for him but without success. His name came up 141 times, none of whom had been born or lived in the Dartford area. I then changed the name to Harold Holloway and this time it came up with 73 matches, none of whom were an exact match. I tried the same two variations against Military Service records and Medal rolls but once again, none were a direct match.

During the First World War there were some 16,000 men who were officially classified as conscientious objectors, 7,000 of whom ended up serving in the military in non-combative role, such as stretcher bearers. Thousands more were sent to prison or labour camps for their beliefs and forty-one were sentenced to death for refusing to carry out any kind of war time service.

CHAPTER SEVEN

Dartford's War Hospitals

Dartford had its fair share of hospitals which were used for military purposes during the First World War.

Dartford War Hospital was split in to two parts. In 1918 the part known as the Upper Southern Hospital was taken over by the United States Government for the use of sick and wounded American officers and soldiers who had been fighting on the Western Front. Officially it became American Base Hospital No.37, and was the largest American Military hospital in England. It had originally started out in July 1917 at the Kings County Hospital in Brooklyn, New York City, but wasn't mobilized and called into service for another year until 18 July 1918. The unit arrived in the UK at Liverpool on 19 May 1918 before travelling on, firstly to the American Rest Camp at Southampton, and then on to Camp Efford in Plymouth which was originally intended to be its permanent location.

The original brick buildings at the Dartford Hospital had been added to in the shape of large wooden huts, which made up most of the wards,

The Dartford Southern Hospital.

each of which could hold up to 100 men. The medical staff, who were all Americans, consisted of 50 surgeons, 100

The Dartford Southern Hospital.

nurses and 200 enlisted men, who worked as orderlies.

King George V, in full military uniform, and in company with Queen Mary, visited the hospital on 20 October 1918 where they were greeted by American Colonel H.E. Fiske and his staff, both military and nursing. This was the first time that the King and Queen had ever visited an American Base Hospital. The Royal couple were shown round the hospital and had the opportunity to speak to some of the wounded and convalescing American soldiers and officers. As they strolled through the grounds they were followed by an ever-increasing crowd of military officers, wounded soldiers and nurses. Some of the men had even had their beds moved out into the grounds. As the King passed he stopped to speak to one of the wounded men who was lying in his bed, going as far as to move the bed sheets back to look at the soldier's injured legs. From the looks of what the men were wearing, thick army coats with woollen hats pulled down over their ears, it must have been an extremely cold day.

There were Union Jack flags adorning the outside of the hospital buildings to add to the historic occasion, with all of the patients and staff appearing to be just as happy to be filmed as they were to meet the King and Queen.

The Americans left soon after the end of the war, on 21 January 1919 when the last of the sick and wounded servicemen returned home to the US. The hospital staff had nursed, nurtured and repaired a total of 4,437 American soldiers, during its relatively short life as a base hospital, of whom forty had died. Most of these fatalities weren't as a result of German bullets or bombs but by contracting influenza.

Dartford Southern Hospital RAMC Band.

With the Americans gone, the hospital reverted to dealing with infectious diseases as well as becoming a convalescent hospital for some of London's poor and needy children.

Throughout the war the part of the site that was referred to as the Lower Southern Hospital, was set aside for seriously wounded German prisoners of war.

The Lower Southern Section of the hospital.

Thousands of Germans were treated there and once they had sufficiently recovered after having their wounds tended to, they were sent to nearby PoW camps. There was one in the town at an old cement works as well as an internment camp within the hospital grounds. Despite the excellent medical facilities and treatment that they received, some prisoners were so badly injured that they did not survive and were buried in the hospital grounds.

It was not an uncommon sight for the residents of Dartford to see convoys of wounded German prisoners arriving at the hospital as well as walking round the town or working on nearby farms. It must have been difficult at times having wounded German and American troops on the same site as well as Australian and British wounded in other parts of the town.

A total of 285 German and Austrian men, who were either patients at the hospital or prisoners at the internment camp, died whilst staying there and were buried in the grounds of the nearby Darenth Park Hospital. They

The Lower Southern Section of the hospital.

Soldiers from the
Royal Army
Medical Corps.

remained there until 1965 when their bodies were exhumed and moved to the German military cemetery at Cannock Chase in Staffordshire.

The man standing on the far right in the back row was Private 23435 John Dunphy who was 22 years old when the photograph was taken. After he had finished his training at the Lower Southern Hospital Dartford, he was sent out to France, where he arrived in time to see action during the Battle of the Somme.

He was born in Whickham in County Durham in 1893. Before the war he had been a miner, a job he went back to after the war. The 1911 Census showed that he lived at Cinderburners Row, Marley Hill, Swalwell, County Durham with his parents, Patrick and Mary Dunphy, and his five brothers James, Thomas, Patrick, Michael, Mathew, and three sisters, Kate, Elizabeth and Mary.

He worked at the local colliery at Marley Hill along with his father

German Prisoners of War at the Lower Southern Hospital.

and three elder brothers James, Thomas and Patrick. His two remaining brothers were still at school in 1911.

I could find no army service records for his three elder brothers, which could mean that they were not called up to serve in the armed forces, which wouldn't have been surprising as they were all miners which was seen as a protected occupation. The importance of providing coal for the continued war effort and the general population was not to be underestimated. It is known, however, that Thomas Dunphy served in the Royal Navy during the war.

John's sister Elizabeth, married a local man, Michael Brough, who also lived in Marley Hill and worked in the same colliery as John. He enlisted in the 13th Battalion, Durham Light Infantry and was awarded the Distinguished Conduct Medal during the actions at Munster Alley and Le Sars.

John Dunphy married Ann Manley, also from County Durham, after he was demobbed from the army in 1919. He died in 1969 aged 76, having never spoken about his war time service and the horrors which he had witnessed.

The Orchard Hospital in Dartford was built in 1902 as temporary premises by the Metropolitan Asylums Board on the banks of the River Thames at Long Reach, to help with the smallpox epidemic that was sweeping the country at the time. It catered for 800 patients. Once the epidemic was over the hospital was closed but still maintained so that it could be re-opened at short notice in the case of another major outbreak.

In 1915 the British Government took possession of the Orchard Hospital, which was near to Joyce Green Aerodrome, for the use of sick and wounded soldiers, but on 9 August 1916 it was made available to the Australians and became the (Dartford) 3rd Australian Auxiliary Hospital under the control of Lieutenant Colonel H. Arthur Powell.

Initially the hospital would have looked very drab and dreary in appearance to its new Australian inhabitants. However, with the help of some good old fashioned elbow grease and a spot of paint, it was soon fully up and running. Over time improvements and additions were made in the shape of a fully functional operating theatre and an increase in the bed capacity to 1,200. There was gas lighting for each of the wards as well as hot water.

The hospital was specifically for the treatment of psychoneuroses

Staff of the Dartford Australian Hospital.

and what, in 1916, were referred to as mental disorders such as shell shock, which required specialist treatment. It was an ailment which had only come about as a result of the First World War when soldiers had to cope with sustained and continuous artillery bombardments, which in some cases would go on for days.

Each of the men admitted to the hospital required intense and prolonged treatment which wasn't always possible for the medical staff to achieve, as they were constantly fighting against the 'six months policy' in which time, if the men's minds hadn't been repaired, they were expected to be invalided back to Australia.

By 31 December 1918 the hospital had taken in a total of 56,411 patients whilst at the same time having discharged 55,527. On 1 January 1919, there were only 884 patients still being treated there.

Some Australians never returned to their homeland after the war but instead chose to stay in the UK having married local women.

Because Dartford had such a glut of hospitals, it was able to set aside some of these sites for military purposes once the war had begun. Its close proximity to the River Thames and London, helped make it a prime location for these much needed medical facilities.

The main gates to Orchard Military Hospital.

CHAPTER EIGHT

East Hill Cemetery – Dartford

The first burial at East Hill Cemetery, or rather Brent Cemetery, as it was originally called, took place on 5 October 1856 when a lady by the name of Elizabeth Barnes was laid to rest on the picturesque 6-acre site.

During the First World War twenty-seven British servicemen were buried at East Hill Cemetery. The bodies of soldiers who died on foreign soil during the war were not brought back home to be buried in their local cemetery as they are today; instead they were buried close to where they had fallen or had died of their wounds; so to have this many soldiers buried at East Hill Cemetery is unusual. This means that they were either badly wounded whilst fighting in one of the many theatres of war and were brought back to England, to have their wounds treated, and then subsequently died, or passed away as a result of an illness or accident such as influenza or an aircraft crash.

They are listed here by the date and year order in which they died.

1915

The first to be buried was **Private C.E. Flack** (NR/20253) 5th Battalion, Queen's Own (Royal West Kent Regiment), who died on 11 February 1915.

Private G.G. Yule (M2/048199), 136th Mechanical Transport Company, Army Service Corps, died on 9 March 1915.

Private Ernest May (3894), 15th The King's Hussars died on 3 June 1915 aged 35. His parents, James and Elizabeth May, lived at 47

Cedar Road, Dartford. He was born in Crayford, enlisted at Maidstone and was a resident of Dartford. He was awarded both the British War Medal as well as the Victory Medal for his service.

Private W.D. Chittenden (NR/20237) 5th Battalion, Queen's Own (Royal West Kent Regiment), died on 17 November 1915.

Private Albert E. Carpenter (CH/13901), Royal Marine Light Infantry, attached to HMS *Calliope*, died on 12 December 1915 at the age of 39. He was born in Meerut in India in 1877, suggesting that he came from a military family. The Commonwealth War Graves Commission (CWGC) website, which did not start compiling its records until the early 1920s, shows Albert's mother, Mrs S. Carpenter, living at 20 Ernest Road, Chatham, Kent.

The 1911 Census shows Albert living at the same address with his wife, Ada and Frederick Knapp who was Ada's brother. Frederick would also become one of the war's casualties – more about him later in this chapter. He was already serving in the military with the Royal Marine Light Infantry at that time.

HMS *Calliope* was a C class light cruiser of the Royal Navy, built at Chatham Dockyard and launched on 17 December 1914. She would go on to take part in the Battle of Jutland in 1916, where she was damaged and ten of her crew were killed.

Rifleman W. Fishwick (20508), 5th Supernumerary Company, 2nd/5th Battalion, The King's (Liverpool) Regiment, died on 27 December 1915.

1916

Bombardier Edward Bird (15879), 40 Brigade, Royal Horse Artillery and Royal Field Artillery, was wounded on the Western Front as a result of gas inhalation and sent back to the UK for hospital treatment where he died on 19 March 1916, aged 21.

He was born in Dartford in 1895 and enlisted at nearby Woolwich. His parents, George and Alice Bird, lived at 115 Westgate Road, Dartford. According to the 1911 Census, Edward was already in the Royal Field Artillery, having enlisted the year he turned eighteen, and living at Woolwich Barracks. He first arrived in France on 18 March 1915 and was awarded the 1915 Star, the British War Medal and the Victory Medal for his wartime service with the colours.

Private Pharoah Feathers (4403), 3rd Battalion, The Loyal North Lancashire Regiment, was born in Bradford, Yorkshire in 1871 and was 40 years of age when he enlisted for one year's service in the Army Reserve (Special Reservists), in Accrington on 30 September 1914. He had previously served with the same regiment before the war according to his Attestation form.

Fortunately his army service record for the First World War has survived so we know quite a bit about the man. He came down to the Dartford area from Accrington in February 1914 and began working at the Vickers Munitions factory on 11 February 1914. Whilst in the area he was living at Colville House, Cold Blow, Sidcup, Kent, which was accommodation for the munitions workers. His wife, Annie, whom he married on 8 June 1898 in St Peter's Church, Accrington, stayed behind in the family home.

Pharoah died of pneumonia at 12.10pm on 19 March 1916 at Dartford Hospital. His wife Annie, who lived at 127 Richmond Street, Accrington, was awarded a pension after his death of 12s 6d a week, commencing 18 September 1916.

Serjeant A.J. Grubb (NR/20061), the Queen's Own (Royal West Kent Regiment), was 56 when he died on 11 May 1916. His widow, Rosa Julia Grubb, lived at 159 Wood Street, Walthamstow.

Rifleman Stewart (or Stuart) Victor Harden (5203), 18th Battalion, London Regiment (London Irish Rifles), was 19 years old when he died of his wounds on 10 July 1916 at the military hospital at Netley near Southampton. The likelihood is that he was injured during the Battle of the Somme and sent back to the UK to have his wounds dealt with, but unfortunately did not pull through. He was born in Rolvenden, Kent in 1897.

According to the 1901 Census, Stewart's parents, Frank Charles and Elizabeth Harden, lived at 49 Staple Street, Hernhill, Kent and had two other children, Frank Junior (5) and Daisy May who was only five months old. Frank senior worked as a carpenter and joiner.

At the time of the 1911 Census the family were still living in the same road but had moved to 5 Staple Street and had three additional children – Charles (5), Iline or Eileen? (5) and one-year-old Olive.

There is an interesting story concerning Stewart. When he was just

18 years of age he initially enlisted on a Short Service Attestation on 7 January 1914 at Woolwich as a gunner (468) in the 139th Battery, Royal Field Artillery. When he enlisted he was already serving with the 5th Battalion, Royal West Kent Regiment, a Territorial Unit, which he had joined on 22 July 1913 as a private (1706) when he was 17 1/2 years of age.

On 11 February, just thirty-five days later, Stewart's military career was over after he was discharged from the service for 'not being likely to become an efficient soldier in line with King's Regulations 392 iii (c)'.

It was more likely that there was an issue surrounding his physical fitness or health, as it is extremely unlikely that a determination as to whether or not he would have become an efficient soldier could have possibly been arrived at in only four weeks. By now his parents had moved to number 98 St Green Street, Dartford.

Stewart was obviously a very brave and determined individual as he managed to re-enlist in the army, a decision that ultimately cost him his life.

Gunner Thomas Reeves (55548), 'C' Battery, 95 Brigade, Royal Field Artillery, died of his wounds on 13 July 1916 aged 19 probably as a result of injuries sustained during the Battle of the Somme. He arrived in France on 9 September 1915 which entitled him to the 1915 Star. His mother lived at 5 Bailey Road, Dartford.

Private Thomas Napper (23329), 120th Protection Company, Royal Defence Corps, died on 3 November 1916. He had previously been a private (21040) in the Sussex Regiment.

Private Joseph Martin (22523), 119th Protection Company, Royal Defence Corps, died on 19 November 1916. He was 52 years of age.

Corporal L.H. Tucker (14777), 4th Battalion, The Coldstream Guards, died of his wounds on 5 December 1916. He was 22 years old. His parents, Thomas Henry and Alice Matilda Tucker, lived at Canal House, Bloomfield Road, Maida Hill, London.

Private John Samuel Jill (29580), 7th Protection Company, Royal Defence Corps, was a London lad having been born in Marylebone.

He died on 23 December 1916. He had previously served as private 20462 in the Somerset Light Infantry.

1917

Private Albert J. Waters (T/1270), 5th Battalion, Queen's Own (Royal West Kent Regiment), was 21 years of age when he died on 22 January 1917.

According to the 1911 Census, his parents, William and Jane Waters, lived with Albert at 30 Little Queen Street, Dartford. They had him late in life, Jane being 49 years old before he was born. Albert was 15 years old, having been born in Woolwich in 1896. He had left school and, like his father, was a general labourer.

On 24 February 1912, aged just 17 years and one month, he enlisted at Dartford, signing on for a period of four years as a private. He was medically discharged from the army on 18 May 1915 at the Royal Victoria Hospital at Netley in Hampshire, for being 'No longer physically fit for war service'. He had served his country for a total of three years and eighty-four days.

Soon after the outbreak of the war Albert's battalion, which was a Territorial Unit, travelled to India to replace one of the regiment's regular and more experienced battalions so that they could be diverted to France. Albert arrived in India on 29 October 1914 and remained there for five months, before arriving back in England on 29 March 1915. His army service record provides an explanation as to why he returned home so quickly, it would appear that whilst serving in India he had contracted tuberculosis, and less than two months later on 18 May 1915, he was medically discharged from the army after being released from Netley hospital in Hampshire and returned to his family, who by now had moved a short distance to 6 Little Green Street.

Less than two years later, on 22 January 1917, Albert was dead, yet another victim of the war.

Private William Privett (22636), 102nd Protection Company, Royal Defence Corps, was 50 years of age when he died on 10 March 1917. He had served in the Egyptian Campaign.

His family lived in Church Street, Ropley, near Alresford, Hampshire. There was his wife Sarah Jane, sons William and Charles, who also served in the army during the war, as well a daughter, Edith, who at 14 was the youngest in the family.

Charles, who had been a grocer's assistant before the war, originally joined the Queen's (Royal West Surrey) Regiment as a private when he enlisted at Winchester on 12 May 1915. He transferred to the 6th Battalion, 369th Company, Labour Company on 3 May 1917 as a private (162796), after having served for nine months in France between 27 July 1915 and 30 April 1916. He returned to England on 1 May and, after sitting before a medical board, he was discharged from the army as no longer being physically fit for war service.

Charles's brother William, who was two years older, was a corporal (G/1150) in the 7th Battalion, Queen's (Royal West Surrey) Regiment. He was killed in action on 28 September 1916 on the Western Front and is commemorated on the Thiepval Memorial on the Somme.

On 28 September 1916 during the Battle of the Somme, the 7th Battalion, Royal West Surrey Regiment joined 53 Infantry Brigade in the attack on the Schwaben Redoubt. They began their attack at 1pm. By the end of the day their casualties included 11 officers and 384 men either killed, wounded or missing. William was unfortunately one of the day's casualties.

It had certainly been a difficult war for Sarah Jane Privett, losing both her husband and her eldest son in the space of just six months.

Private Thomas Mark Dillaway (8078), Royal Army Medical Corps, was born in Dartford in 1896, enlisting in the army at the start of the war, aged 18, on 6 August 1914 in Woolwich. When he died of tuberculosis on 23 August 1917 at his grandmother's house, 38 Mount Pleasant Road, Dartford, he was just 21 years of age.

Having undertaken and completed his basic training at Aldershot he left for foreign climes, arriving in Egypt on 6 November 1915 returning to England on 30 August 1916. Two weeks later on 11 September 1916 he was sitting in front of an Army Medical Board in London, concerning the diagnosis of his medical condition, 'tubercle of the lung', which in Thomas's case was so severe that the decision for the board was a relatively straightforward one. He was medically discharged from the army as no longer fit for war service.

He had been released from Tooting Military Hospital on 21 September 1916, but after briefly visiting his grandmother and his three sisters who all lived with her, he was the very next day admitted to the Brompton Hospital for Consumption in Fulham Road, south-west London.

He was officially discharged from the army on 25 September 1916 and provided with a pension of 25/- shillings a week, which was only to last for a period of six months.

1918

Lieutenant George Thomas Bodycomb was a temporary second lieutenant in the Royal Flying Corps when he died on 18 February 1918. There is a comprehensive entry about George in the chapter on the Dartford War Memorial.

Private Herbert Benjamin Prue (D/8499), 4th Battalion, Dragoon Guards (The Princess Royal's) Hertfordshire Yeomanry, was born in Dartford in 1895 and on 17 November 1913 aged 18, he enlisted in the army. He died on 13 September 1918 aged 23.

Whilst serving in Egypt Herbert was involved in the following incident which resulted in his sustaining a fractured metatarsal to his left foot and a visit to the local hospital.

'TO O/C CAVALRY SCHOOL OF INSTRUCTION.
Report on accident to No.8499 L/Cpl. Prue H.B.
On the morning of Tuesday 5th Feb. my class under Major Northern, was carrying out a scheme to illustrate intercommunication.
Captain Taylor and myself were working together and on completion rode to the pumping station I dismounted and handed my horse over to L/Cpl Prue. Capt. Taylor rode off with a message to Captain Woodhouse.
I was sitting down studying a map when I heard a heavy kick and on looking round saw that L/Cpl. Prue was in pain. I took the horses off him and tied them up & returned and took off his boot, cut away his sock and found he had been severely kicked on the instep. I then got into communication with O/room informed them of the accident and asked for a car to be sent along for L/Cpl. Prue. The accident was entirely accidental & happened in the execution of his duty.

Signed H. Spencer Lt 7th A L H Regt.'

Herbert added his own written account of the incident some five days later on 12 February 1918.

'Sir, I was on duty, as orderly to an Australian officer, at Cairo Pumping Station, on the 5th Feb. We were dismounted, I holding the two horses. My own horse took fright at something and jumped forward. The mare's hind foot coming down on my left foot.

Signed 8499 L/Cpl. Prue
    Substantiated by H, Spencer Bt. 7th L H Herts Yeo. Att TSI'

Herbert had first arrived in France on 31 November 1915 which, besides other awards, qualified him for the 1915 Star. He was there for just over a year, returning home on Christmas Day 1916. He remained in the UK until 12 April 1917 when he once again returned to France, but he was only there for eleven weeks before arriving in Egypt on 1 July 1917 as part of the Egyptian Expeditionary Force, where he remained for the next year before returning to the UK on 19 June 1918.

The 1911 Census showed a 13-year-old Herbert living with his parents, Benjamin Thomas and Betsy Prue, his elder brother, Thomas and his two sisters, Bessie and Harriet, at 63 Colney Road, Dartford, Kent. Herbert's army service record clearly shows the address as being 53 Colney Road.

Having survived fighting in both France and Egypt he was discharged from the army on 7 September 1918, after nearly five years, diagnosed as being no longer physically fit for war service due to having diabetes. Only nine days later Herbert was dead. The army was informed of his death by a letter from Herbert's father.

'TO THE OFFICER OF RECORDS.
Sir, I am writing to inform you that my son Herbert Benjamin Prue 8499 1st Herts Yeomanry passed away on Saturday morning at 9.20am. He was sent home to us from Birmingham on Aug 20th suffering from diabetes. He has been a great worry and trouble to us since then. We have had a nurse with him night and day and also to have him on special diet. All this has been a great deal of

expense for me and being only a working man think that I am
entitled to some little compensation.
Yours faithfully
   B.J. Prue'

When a soldier's army service record has survived like Herbert's has, it is a window in time which allows so much more about them to become known, not just as a soldier but as a human being; it helps to bring their individual stories to life.

Herbert had two entries on his company conduct sheet, both incidents occurring when he was stationed at Tidworth Barracks. The first occasion took place on 7 September 1914 at 0315 hours when he was found asleep whilst carrying out sentry duty. This so angered his commanding officer that he was sentenced to fourteen days detention.

The following year on 14 May 1915 he was absent from duty for two days, the reason why was not explained, but his punishment was simply a verbal reprimand.

Either of those offences, if committed in France or Belgium, would have more than likely seen Herbert facing a court martial, and if found guilty his punishment may have been a firing squad, especially as they were both early on in the war when senior officers were mindful of setting an example to discourage such behaviour.

Farrier Serjeant Ernest Henry Baulk (686831), Royal Field Artillery, died on 13 November 1918. There is a comprehensive entry about Ernest in the chapter on the Dartford War Memorial.

Pioneer Frederick Thomas Parker (375238), Royal Engineers, died of influenza aged 29, on 15 November 1918, just four days after the war had ended. He left behind a widow, Emma.

1919

Rifleman Frederick William Wilson (591784), 18th Battalion, London Regiment (London Irish Rifles), died on 16 February 1919. He was 26 years old. His parents, John and Eliza Wilson, lived in Chelsea in London and he left a widow, Caroline.

Gunner G. Humble (93522), Royal Garrison Artillery, died on 17 April 1919. He was 35 years of age and a local man from Dartford.

Driver William Stevens (60961), 'A' Battery, 285 Brigade, Royal Field Artillery, enlisted at Woolwich on 4 January 1915. After having completed his initial training and pre-deployment preparation, he arrived in France with his regiment on 28 September 1915.

His disciplinary record was not a particularly impressive one. He had only been there for two weeks when his problems began and he was docked five day's pay for 'hesitating to obey an order'. Over time he added further fines to his record by being 'late on parade', 'absent from roll call', and for being 'improperly dressed on parade'.

He died of sickness on 7 August 1919 whilst a patient at the Dartford Livingstone Cottage Hospital. He had only been demobbed from the army on 20 May 1919 after completing his wartime service. He was 21 years of age.

According to the 1911 Census, William had three brothers and three sisters. His brother Henry was four years older, but I could find no record of him having served during the war. When William died his parents, Amos and Elizabeth Stevens, who lived at 44 St Vincents Road, Dartford, wrote to the army asking if their son was entitled to a military funeral. They were informed that he was not but that the army would pay for the cost of the funeral, which must have been a big help for the family.

1920

Private Charles Nicholas Mann (TR9/7223), 52nd Battalion, Bedfordshire Regiment died on 26 January 1920. He left a widow, May Lilian Mann, who lived at 2 Marriot Road, Dartford. Unfortunately his army service record has not survived, so finding out anything about how he died has proved to be a fruitless search.

Shoeing Smith Fred Knapp (35448), Royal Field Artillery, died on 15 October 1920 aged 39.

Fred had enlisted in the army on 7 December 1900 at the age of 20, and was posted to Gosport to undergo his initial training. He originally signed on for three years although he went on to serve for nineteen years and four months before retiring at his own request on 15 April 1920, entitling him to an 'eighteen years pension'. Having reached eighteen years' service on 22 February 1918, he signed on for a further three years to take him to twenty-one years' service.

He served in South Africa during the Second Boer War and was then stationed in India between 3 October 1903 and 11 March 1908. He also served in France as well as Palestine during the First World War.

He married Amy Frances Bulton, a widow with a 5-year-old daughter, Winifred. They married on 11 June 1919 whilst he was still serving in the army.

Although Fred's Army pension record survived, his army service record did not, so we still do not know how it was that he came to die at such a relatively young age.

CHAPTER NINE

Dartford – Watling Street Cemetery

Dartford Watling Street Cemetery.

The land which is now home to Watling Street Cemetery was acquired in 1900 by the Dartford Urban District Council to provide local residents with an area where they could bury their loved ones.

The first person to be buried there was a Mr James Duggan who was laid to rest on Tuesday, 7 April 1914. The chapel which stands in the grounds of the cemetery, held its first service on 7 December 1916, soon after its construction was completed.

Twenty-seven soldiers and airmen who lost their lives as a result of the First World War are buried in the cemetery. Their names are recorded alphabetically.

As many service records from the First World War were destroyed during German bombing raids over London during the Second World War, it has not been possible, other than some very basic facts, to find out much about all of the servicemen who are buried there.

Five were members of the Royal Flying Corps No. 63 Training Squadron, all of whom were killed in flying accidents whilst they were stationed at Joyce Green Aerodrome, showing just how dangerous training to be a pilot was, let alone being an operational flyer engaging in dog fights.

Gunner F. Balchin (63692),156th Heavy Battery of the Royal Garrison Artillery, died of wounds on 2 November 1918, just nine days before the Armistice. He was 34 years of age.

Gunner Frank Barnes (194860), Royal Horse Artillery and Royal Artillery, was born in Dartford and enlisted at nearby Woolwich. He died of his wounds on 8 October 1918 aged 19. His home was at 15 West Hill, Dartford, a place he shared with ten other people. Head of the household was his mother Lucy Barnes, his four brothers, a sister, three cousins, along with a 47-year-old boarder, Joseph Thomas Foster.

Only one of Frank's brothers would have been old enough to serve in the army and that was John who was 23 years old at the outbreak of the war. There was no military service record for John, but the 1911 Census shows him as being employed as a labourer at a Gelatine Works, so it is more than likely that he had an exemption from war service because of his job.

Arthur Thomas Exeter was one of the cousins who lived with the family and he was just a year younger than Frank's elder brother, John. They worked in the same Gelatine Works as labourers, and despite this Arthur did end up in the army. Whether that was because he enlisted voluntarily or was called up is not known. He ended up as a Lance Serjeant (R/23990) in the 18th Battalion, King's Royal Rifle Corps. He was a truly remarkable young man, who was awarded the Military Medal on three occasions for his acts of bravery as well as being mentioned in despatches.

Unfortunately Arthur did not survive the war. He died of his wounds on 22 October 1918 whilst serving in France. He is buried in the Lijssenthoek Military Cemetery at Poperinghe, Belgium.

Lijssenthoek Military Cemetery. (Commonwealth War Graves Commission)

The 18th (Arts & Crafts) Battalion, King's Royal Rifle Corps was formed at Gidea Park, Romford on 4 June 1915 by Sir Herbert Raphael. After they had completed their initial training in Aldershot and Witley, they landed at Le Havre in France on 3 May 1916. The battalion moved to Italy in November 1917, but stayed only a short while before returning to France in March 1918 where they remained until the end of the war.

Leading Stoker Thomas H. Bates (SS/111411), Royal Navy was attached to HMS Lennox when he died of an unspecified illness, possibly pneumonia, on 27 October 1918.

HMS *Lennox* was a Laforey Class destroyer launched just five months before the outbreak of war. She was attached to the Harwich Force. During the war a priority of the Royal Navy was to secure the approaches to the English Channel from ships of the German Fleet, which was the job of such units as the Harwich Force which consisted of between four and eight light cruisers and between thirty to forty destroyers.

Private Alfred Henry Blackman (G/483), 6th Battalion, The Buffs (East Kent Regiment), was born in Darenth, Kent in 1894. He was a month away from his twenty-first birthday when he enlisted in the army on 31 August 1914 at Woolwich. He was initially posted to Canterbury to begin his military training. Whilst still in the UK he was admitted to the Suffolk Hospital in Bury St Edmunds between 18 March and 5 April 1916 before being admitted to the Red Cross Hospital at Sussex Lodge in Newmarket three days later on 8 April. He remained in the UK until 21 June 1916, before landing in France the following day.

Alfred's army pension record is slightly confusing because it shows that he was gassed on 1 September 1916 and wounded again only nine days later on 14 September 1916 when he received gunshot wounds to his right arm, his right leg and his back, suggesting that the incident when he was gassed had not been too severe.

He was discharged from the army on 7 April 1917 as no longer fit for war service due to having had his left arm amputated. At the time of his discharge he had been transferred to the 1st Battalion of The Buffs. His wartime service earned him the 1915 Star, the British War Medal as well as the Victory Medal.

On leaving the army Alfred lived at 30 Durmont Road, Stoke Newington, London, N16 and was awarded a pension, initially of 27s 6d for nine weeks, thereafter reduced to 16s 6d, for life. He died on 12 November 1919 aged 26.

His parents, Alfred and Lily May Blackman, lived at 19 Howard Road, Dartford with their two other sons, Sydney and William, who on 1 July 1920 were aged 14 and 9 years of age respectively. They also had seven daughters.

Gunner C. Chidwick (RMA/6522), 'C' Company, Royal Marine Artillery, served with the surname of Leon. He died on 7 September 1919. His parents, William and Sonny Chidwick, lived in Goring, Sussex. There was no military service record for anybody with the surname of either Chidwick or Leon who had served with the Royal Marine Artillery.

Second Lieutenant Allan Gladstone Dow, Royal Flying Corps and the General List, was only 21 years old when he was killed in a flying accident on 17 August 1917. His Medal Index Card shows a strange entry. Somebody has hand written 'Killed 17-8-17'. The word 'killed' has at a later time been crossed through and replaced with 'drowned'.

His parents, John and Alice Dow, lived at 607 O'Connor Street, Ottowa, Canada.

Gunner F. Hodge (40419), No.1 Reinforcement Siege Depot, Royal Garrison Artillery, died on 2 December 1918.

Lieutenant Jean-Charles Romauld Leduc, Royal Flying Corps, was a Canadian from Ottawa. He was 21 years old when he was killed on 7 November 1917.

His parents, Clovis and Angelina Leduc, lived at 153 Nepean Street, Ottawa, Canada, although Jean-Charles was born at St Henry in Montreal.

Second Lieutenant Harry Hall Gunther, Royal Air Force, was another Canadian. He was only 19 years old when he died on 18 July 1918. He was a member of No. 63 Training Squadron, in the newly renamed Royal Air Force, which was formed on 29 March 1917 at Turnhill and beside other aircraft, flew Avros, Sopwith Pups and Sopwith Camels. It was dedicated to scout training and for a time had operated out of Joyce Green Aerodrome, which would explain why so many from the squadron are buried at Dartford's Watling cemetery.

His father, Julius Harry Gunther, lived in Listowel, Ontario, Canada.

Rifleman C. Mahon, 12th Battalion, The Rifle Brigade, was a 35-year-old married man who lived at 66 Invicta Road, Stone, Dartford. He enlisted on 26 April 1915 and was medically discharged for being physically unfit for war service on 9 May 1917. He died of his wounds nearly a year later on 4 April 1918.

The battalion was raised in September 1914 at Winchester and came under the command of 60 Brigade in the 20th (Light) Division. They initially went to camp at Blackdown, moving on to Witley in February 1915, Larkhill two months later, before arriving in Boulogne on 22 July 1915.

Lieutenant Wilfred Graham Salmon, Royal Flying Corps Special Reserve, was from Ballarat in Victoria, Australia. He died on 7 July 1917. He was awarded the 1915 Star, the British War Medal and the Victory Medal.

Private David John Rohan (284921), 601st Home Service Company, Labour Corps, died aged 40 on 28 February 1919. The entry on the

British Army First World War Medal Rolls Index Cards is slightly confusing in so far as it shows that he was discharged from the army on 28 February 1919. He had previously been a private (11998) in the Duke of Edinburgh's (Wiltshire Regiment).

Serjeant W.H. Frank March (16893), 63 Training Squadron, Royal Air Force, was killed on 24 April 1918.

Serjeant William Potter (TF/240065 & 1092), Queen's Own (Royal West Kent Regiment), was killed on 15 April 1919.

Captain C.R.J. Thompson, 63 Training Squadron, Royal Air Force, was killed on 17 July 1918.

Sapper J.L. Ridgewell (541960), 20th Territorial Force Depot, Royal Engineers, died on 7 January 1919. The unit was located in Pier Road, Gillingham, Kent and the role appeared to be a purely administrative one, with such units typically having a strength of about one officer and ten soldiers. Men were quite often attached to these units when they were either being treated in hospital or recuperating at home.

Private Frederick Charles Thrussell (3596), 3rd Battalion, 15th Hussars, Reserve Cavalry Regiment, died on 25 February 1921. He had first arrived in France soon after the outbreak of the war on 16 August 1914 which entitled him to the 1914 Star as well as the British War Medal and the Victory Medal.

Corporal Thomas O'Connor was born in Lambeth in 1883 and had first enlisted in the army on 13 March 1901 in London, during the time of the Second Boer War in South Africa, signing on for twelve years. He was not yet 19 years of age. Immediately prior to this he had been serving with the 3rd Battalion, East Surrey Regiment, which was a Militia Unit.

On enlisting in the Regular Army he became a private (6583) in the 1st Garrison Battalion, Devonshire Regiment. He was promoted to the rank of corporal on 1 June 1918 and demobilized on 18 March 1919, having served for just over eighteen years. His address at the time was 20 Howard Road, Dartford.

Thomas had obviously enjoyed his life in the army, re-enlisting in both 1909 and 1913 for four more years on each occasion. He had first arrived in France on 12 September 1914, suggesting that he had either been in the army before the war or he had been a reservist who was called up at the outbreak of the war.

He was awarded the South African Medal for his service in the Boer War (1899-1902), and the 1914 Star, as well as the British War and Victory Medals for his wartime service. He had served in India, Egypt, South Africa and France during his eighteen years in the army, spending most of the First World War in Egypt.

He married Alice O'Halloran at St John's Church in Newington on 1 May 1910. They had two sons, Thomas who was born on 12 April 1911 in West Ham and Terence who was born on 28 August 1914 in Dartford.

Thomas died on 17 April 1921, but his service record does not offer any further explanation as to how he died. For him to be included on the CWGC website suggests that the cause of his death would have been related to his wartime service.

Lance Corporal J. Mitchell (304775), 16th Battalion, Tank Corps died on 15 February 1919. Unfortunately I could not find any other information about him.

Staff Sergeant and Saddler John Hale Williams (T/15326), Army Service Corps, died on 21 January 1920 aged 38. Although Welsh by birth, at the time of his death he lived with his wife Mary at 19 Raeburn Avenue, Dartford. His parents, Thomas and Elizabeth Williams, still lived in Cardiff.

He had originally enlisted in 1902 just after the end of the Second Boer War in South Africa, before going on to serve in the army for eighteen years.

Rifleman Alexander Joseph Tomalin (555927), 9th Battalion, London Regiment (Queen Victoria's Rifles), died on 1 December 1918.

His parents, Alfred and Edith Tomalin, lived at 12 York Road, Dartford. Alexander was the eldest of four children. He had a brother, Hubert, as well as two sisters, Beatrice and Kathleen. Alexander's father Alfred, died in Dartford in December 1952 aged 79.

Private Ernest Edward Waring, 5th Battalion, Queen's Own (Royal West Kent Regiment), died on 17 June 1921 aged 21.

For his name to have been included on the CWGC website, when he died nearly three years after the end of the war, is a strong indicator that his death must have come about as a direct result of an injury or illness which took place during his military service.

Whilst trying to confirm the information about Ernest to ensure that this entry about him was correct, the issue surrounding the accuracy of some historic records came up as if to help highlight this very point. Firstly, keep in mind that the level of literacy amongst the general population was often low in the early 1900s.

We know Ernest's mother's name was Emily Waring as shown on his entry in the CWGC website. This therefore was the starting point. A check on the 1901 Census shows Emily married to Frederick J. Waring, living at 4 Chesterfield Grove, Camberwell, London. They had four children, Olive E.J. (4), Francis J.J. (3), Ernest E. (1) and seven-month old Julia G. The same entry also showed that Frederick was an Electrotyper by way of occupation who was born in St Lukes and was 27 years of age, whilst Emily was 29 and was born in Lambeth.

Jump forward ten years to the 1911 Census and it shows the Waring family living at 8 Kingsfield Terrace, Priory Road, Dartford, but there are a few changes. Frederick now has the name of Frank, who just happens to have the same occupation of Electrotyper and he is 37. Emily is shown as being 39. Frederick and Emily now have six children, the last two being born in 1905 and 1906, after the 1901 Census.

Looking at the four eldest children, there is Olive aged 13. Francis has now become Frank aged 13, which is an accepted variation of the same name, like Steve or Stephen would be. Julia is now 10 and Ernest E. has now become Edward, who is eleven. Maybe Edward was Ernest's middle name.

On the balance of probabilities, I would say that we are talking about the same family and the discrepancies in the two records are simply down to errors caused by those who wrote them. You may however think differently.

After the war Ernest's/Edward's mother, Emily Waring, lived at 'Westcombe', Essex Road, Dartford.

Lieutenant Charles Henry Williams, 63 Training Squadron, Royal Air Force, was killed in a flying accident on 2 August 1918, aged 22.

There is a record of a Second Lieutenant Charles Henry Williams of the Royal Flying Corps having acquired his flying licence at the London and Provincial Flying School in Edgware on 9 June 1917. He was born on 15 September 1895 in Harrogate, Yorkshire,

Lieutenant John Percival Van Ryneveld, 63 Training Squadron, Royal Air Force, died on 2 June 1918.

His father was Daniel Johannes Van Ryneveld from South Africa who was born in 1860. John had a brother Hesperus Andreas Van Ryneveld, who went on to become General Sir Pierre (Nickname) Van Ryneveld who was born on 2 May 1891 in Senegal and who died on 2 December 1972. He had been a pilot in both the Royal Flying Corps and Royal Air Force during the First World War and went on to become the founding commander of the South African Air Force, which he established in 1920, the year in which he was knighted.

As a major he had been the commanding officer of 45 Squadron between 24 April and 18 August 1917.

Second Lieutenant Harold George Tucker, No 5 Training Depot, Royal Air Force Station, Royal Flying Corps, died on 4 April 1918.

Prior to receiving his commission on 5 September 1916 he had been a private (1079/245101) in the Queen's Own Royal West Kent Yeomanry, with which he had served in the Balkans theatre of war, first arriving there on 8 October 1915. Besides the British War Medal and the Victory Medal, he also qualified for the 1915 Star.

He was a married man and when his wife applied for his wartime medals on 17 August 1922, she was living at 1 Dryden Mansions, Queens Club Gardens, London W14.

Second Lieutenant Charles Herbert Wheelock, Royal Flying Corps and General List, was 25 years old when he died on 19 March 1918 in Dartford. He may have been stationed at the nearby Joyce Green Aerodrome, which was both an operational flying base as well as a training station during the First World War. It was also used by Vickers Ltd to design, manufacture and test new aircraft, as well as being a Wireless Testing Centre.

On the British Army Medal Rolls Index Cards for the First World War, there is a Charles H. Wheelock who is shown as having being a Gunner (83774) in the Canadian Field Artillery. It also shows that he was a second lieutenant in the Royal Flying Corps and that although he had served in France, having arrived there on 14 September 1915, he died in the UK on 17 March 1918.

Engine Fitter Arthur Sidney West (1014) was in the Australian Munition Workers service when he died 8 November 1917. He was 27 years of age, born on 26 June 1889 in Enfield in Sydney, Australia. His parents, William and Mary West, lived at 'Plymouth' Punchbowl Road, Enfield, Sydney, New South Wales.

Arthur has a very interesting story. At the outbreak of the First World War he was deemed to be unfit for military service so he came over to England to specifically work in a munitions factory and to do his bit for the war effort.

On 6 November 1916 during the voyage from Australia to England, his ship, the P&O liner, *Arabia*, was sunk by a torpedo fired from a German U-boat, off Cape Matapan in Greece. Thankfully, most of the passengers and crew on board the *Arabia*, including Arthur, survived.

When he eventually arrived in England he was sent to work at the Vickers Munitions factory at Crayford in Kent. On 8 November 1917 whilst he was working in the Rifle Stock department, he was killed in what can only be described as a tragic accident when he fell in to a band-cutting machine and subsequently died from internal haemorrhaging.

The factory at Crayford had their own magazine which published the following article about Arthur:

'As a mechanic he was keen, energetic and thorough. As a man and a comrade he was appraised by all who knew him. In the midst of any worry he was always well met and his smile so nearly approached permanency that he appealed to all as the personification of content.

Only 28 years of age, in the bloom of manhood and under extremely ghastly and unfortunate circumstances, he met his death as a true born soldier, in the course and execution of his duty. He was buried at East Hill Cemetery, Dartford on November 13th 1917.

His friends and fellow Australians accompanied his remains to their last resting place. Many beautiful floral tokens bore tribute to the esteem and affection in which he was held by all. He will ever be remembered and his name will be held sacred by his fellow Australians who will sadly mourn his demise.'

A simple inscription on his grave reads;
  'Erected to his memory by fellow Aussie munition workers
  and friends. Died from injuries received at his work –
  8th November 1917 aged 28 years.'

Arthur Sidney West's grave.

CHAPTER TEN

Stone Cemetery Dartford

Stone Cemetery in Dartford has been in existence for well over a hundred years, taking its first burial on 14 June 1899 when a Mr Robert Goodway was buried there. In the years since then, the number has risen to in excess of 5,000, including eight graves of servicemen from the First World War.

Private Percy Barnden (2804), Royal Army Medical Corps, 5th General Hospital, died on 22 February 1919.

Shoeing Smith/Gunner Arthur Bodle (52565), Royal Garrison Artillery, arrived in France on 30 August 1915. The CWGC website

shows that he died on 30 January 1919.

Besides the British War and Victory Medals, he was also awarded the 1914-15 Star, the criteria for it being for soldiers who saw service in any theatre of war between 5 August 1915 and 31 December 1915, other than those servicemen who had been awarded the 1914 Star.

Thankfully Arthur's army service record has survived. It shows that at the time of his enlistment at Gravesend on 18 November 1914,

Stone Cemetery.

he was a few weeks away from his twenty-first birthday and was living at 57 High Street, Greenhithe, Kent. In January of that year he had married Rose at the Parish Church, Greenhithe. Their first child, a daughter Violet, was born on 12 April 1914, three months later. Their first son Alfred Arthur Albert Bodle was born on 29 May 1915, but died of bronchitis before he was six months old, on 10 November 1915. Their second son, Arthur John Bodle, was born on 29 March 1918.

After Arthur's death, Rose moved and was living at 13 Castle Street in Greenhithe. Like all the soldiers who died during, or as a result of the First World War, Arthur's death was tragic, but his also had a tinge of irony attached to it. He had survived the war, having served in France for more than three years, but then died as a result of a freak accident whilst on demob leave. He fell through a cellar flap at the Tilbury Dock canteen and fractured his skull, an injury from which he died.

Amongst Arthur's army service record is a letter written by Rose, dated 17 March 1919. It was sent to the Royal Garrison Artillery Records office at Dover.

'17/3/19

Sir, In reply to your letter dated 14th March I beg to inform you that my late husband's death took place on the 29th January 1919 in a sad accident at Tilbury. I have sent a report of the accident. Would you kindly send the piece of paper back in the stamped addressed envelope as that is the only one I have to keep. My late husband was buried in the cemetery of Stone parish Greenhithe. He had a Military Funeral from Gravesend Military Barracks.

I am yours faithfully,
Mrs R. Bodle'

It was interesting to note that Arthur's wife said that her husband had died the day before what had actually been recorded as his date of death on his army service record.

After his return to England he stayed in two hospitals after accidentally having injured one of his feet whilst serving in France. From 22 November 1918 to 12 December 1918, he was a patient at the 2nd Western General Hospital in Manchester and from there he was moved to Fort Pitt Dispersal Hospital in Chatham, where he remained until 29 January 1919. His accident took place the day of his discharge from hospital.

Even though Arthur was still a serving soldier at the time of his death, the Minister of Pensions decided that because it was an accident, his widow Rose was not eligible for the grant of any pension. He did however deem it worthy to refer the matter to the Local War Pensions Committee for their consideration.

Private H. Brown (1700), enlisted in the Queen's Own (Royal West Kent Regiment) but was transferred to the Labour Corps where he became private 365776. He died on 4 November 1920 aged 43.

Chief Stoker William Brown (154094), Royal Navy, was part of the crew of HMS *Pembroke* when he died aged 47 on 15 November 1918, just four days after the Armistice was signed. His wife lived at 6 Archers Cottages, Bean, Dartford. His parents, Charles and Jane Brown, who by now were quite elderly, were living at Green Street, Dartford.

R. Charnock (756501) was a cook in the Mercantile Marine Reserve. He died on 15 May 1919 and was one of the crew on HM Tug Boat, *St Aubin* which was a Saint Class boat, one of only four built by Harland and Wolff ship builders at Govan in Scotland in 1918. At the outbreak of the war the Royal Navy had only seven tug boats. To fulfil the need for such boats to carry out a host of basic naval duties, the Admiralty had to requisition over a hundred civilian tugs.

Private Albert Fletcher (982) 'D' Company, 6th Battalion, Queen's Own (Royal West Kent Regiment), enlisted on 1 September 1914 at Gravesend and, after having completed his initial training, he arrived in France on 1 June 1915.

Although his army service record doesn't show the date, he was returned to England due to poor health and admitted to Tooting Military Hospital where he died at 11.30pm on 2 February 1916 from pulmonary and laryngeal tuberculosis. He first reported himself sick with related symptoms in October 1915. He was 28 years of age, although his Medal Rolls Index Card, shows his date of death a day later, on 3 February 1916.

One of his brothers, John William Fletcher, lived at 107 Charles

Street, Stone, Dartford, whilst his other, Charles Edward Fletcher, lived at 176 Charles Street, Chatham. His sister, Florence, also lived at this address.

Private Robert Edward Hibben (651165), 47th Battalion, Canadian Infantry (British Columbia Regiment) died of his wounds aged 20 on 25 September 1918. His parents, Robert and Emma Hibben, lived at Lucknow, Ontario, Canada, but before emigrating had previously lived in Stone, Kent.

Petty Officer/Stoker Walter Frederick Ould (K/6525 CH), Royal Navy was born on 21 February 1892 in Swanscombe, Kent. He died from an unspecified disease on 14 July 1918 aged 26. He was part of the crew on board HMS *Zinnia* which was launched in 1915. She was a Flower class sloop built as part of the Emergency War Programme.

According to the 1911 Census Walter was 19 years old, and was already in the Royal Navy. He was a married man, and his wife Daisy lived at 119 St Albans, Newtown, Dartford.

The 1911 Census shows a Herbert Henry Ould also born in Swanscombe in 1894. It is not known if he was related to Walter, although it is highly likely that he was. Herbert was a private in the Royal Marine Light Infantry and was killed in action on 29 April 1915 at Gallipoli.

CHAPTER ELEVEN

Women in the Great War

The First World War has often been regarded as a significant turning point for women as they were at last given the opportunity to undertake many of the jobs in commerce and industry that had traditionally been the sole domain of men. With hundreds of Dartford men called up for military service, it was up to local women to fill the subsequent gaps.

In the munitions industry women did almost every job available, making and filling shells and cartridges, labouring, cleaning, catering, driving and storeroom-keeping. Much of the work in munitions was repetitive and women were, in the main, employed on automatic or semi-automatic machines. However, they were given the opportunity to learn some skills in engineering, which included the production of many kinds of weapons.

During the First World War, Vickers Ltd was a major employer of women with munitions factories at Erith, Crayford and Dartford. They were noisy environments to work in, as well as being extremely dangerous. The language amongst the men could be vulgar and blunt at times, but most would tone it down if there were women around.

Vickers even had their own hostels for workers to live in who weren't from the local area, including a number of Dutch and other foreign workers. They were well looked after both with the level of accommodation and the quality of the food that was provided.

Women also worked in the transport industry as bus conductors, ticket collectors, porters, carriage cleaners and bus drivers. The Royal Mail recruited a large force of female van drivers; others were trained as carpenters, plumbers and gas fitters. Lots of women wore uniform for the first time as nurses, VAD' (Voluntary Aid Detachment), WAACs (Women's Army Auxiliary Corps) or, in 1917, as members of the newly-formed Women's Land Army. Those who joined the Land Army usually undertook general field work or dairy work, as well as ploughing.

The women of Dartford were no different from women up and down the country; they wanted to do their bit for the war effort in whatever way they could. There weren't many who didn't have a brother, son, husband or father who had gone off to fight in the war. It gave women a sense of purpose as well as freedom and an income which would have otherwise never come their way.

This was a time of the Suffragette movement where women wanted equality and no longer wanted a life based on being a second class citizen. It was the dawning of a brave new world and they wanted to be part of it.

Following the outbreak of the First World War a joint war committee was formed between the Order of St John and the British Red Cross. Its main purpose was to work together to pool resources as well as wartime fund raising efforts. A lot of the work that was carried out was by men and women, from local Voluntary Aid Detachments. Kent provided invaluable additional aid to military forces from both the army and navy during the war.

British Red Cross activities throughout Kent began on 13 August 1914. This included the opening of auxiliary hospitals and the staffing of them with the help of VADs. The first wounded soldiers from the fighting in and around Mons began arriving back in the UK the very next day at Dover. From there they were transferred to hospitals all over Kent. Which hospital they were sent to depended on the extent of their injuries. Dr Cotton, who was the Deputy Commissioner of the St John Ambulance Brigade, as well as the County Director of Territorial Forces Association, became the Kent County Director, in charge of all VAD work throughout the county.

The women of Kent certainly played their part, including those from the Dartford area. At the start of the war forty-eight auxiliary hospitals opened across the county, each requiring nursing staff, most of whom were women. By the end of the war forty-eight had become eighty which helped provide some 4,730 beds for wounded soldiers. Hospitals sprang up all over the place and in all kinds of different buildings. There were village halls, school buildings, clubs and stately homes, all made available for the greater need and the good of the ever-increasing numbers of wounded soldiers, sailors and airmen. In total, between the outbreak of the war in 1914 and the latter half of 1919, more than 125,000 patients were treated in the Kent area. Locally, none of this would have been possible without the dedication and hard work of the women of Dartford and the surrounding areas.

Dartford Hospital staff.

Although nearly every large town throughout the country had VADs as part of their local community, they were centralised and run from Devonshire House, London for most of the war. Most of the women who joined these local VADs did so as nurses, but first they had to successfully complete an extensive nursing course so that they were capable of dealing with the large number of wounded servicemen who were arriving in the UK, mainly from France and Belgium.

Nurse Margaret Maule seen here on the back row, second from the right.

Dartford First World War Nurses.

Although this chapter is about women in the war it is only right to point out that not all VADs were made up entirely of women. There were male detachments as well, made up of those who were either too old or not fit enough to serve in the military. Their main role was the transporting of sick and wounded men from the ambulance trains that arrived at Dartford station, to local hospitals, at anytime of the day or night. There were special field ambulances placed at their disposal which were reserved for what were referred to as 'cot-cases', men who had to be carried by stretcher because of their injuries. Those who could stand and walk were often conveyed to their destination in private cars that had been loaned by affluent members of the community.

The male VADs would also act as orderlies, mainly in the auxiliary hospitals, and as wardens during air raids.

Dartford Workhouse

Like most towns up and down the country, Dartford had its own workhouse. The first purpose built one in Chatham was opened in 1729 and stood at the corner of West Hill and Priory Hill. The workhouse was moved in the mid 1800s to a site that faces onto West Street, and the building still stands to this day.

Workhouses by their very nature were spartan and uninviting places, but for those who were unable to support themselves and didn't have a roof over their heads, there was little or no other option. There was no such thing as the Welfare State before the First World War, so workhouses catered for all elements of society, ranging from the poor, the destitute, the mentally ill, as well as unmarried mothers.

At the outbreak of the First World War, the Dartford workhouse and its hospital were closed and handed over to Vickers Limited, who were involved in providing munitions, mainly artillery shells, for the war effort. The workhouse was urgently needed as accommodation blocks for the hundreds of munition workers that were flooding into the town to work at the Vickers site. The infirmary was used for its original purpose and became a hospital for the munition workers.

CHAPTER TWELVE

War Memorials

War Memorials and church rolls of honour are always an interesting topic because over the years the boundaries of towns, cities and boroughs have changed, in some instances, quite drastically.

For example Fawkham and Hartley both fall within the postal area of Dartford and have 'DA' postcodes, but are actually covered by Sevenoaks District Council, not Dartford Borough Council. Even though the two councils have merged, the only service which they share is that of benefits. So there is always going to be a certain amount of disagreement concerning which town, district or borough certain war memorials or rolls of honour should be a part of. I mention this in the hope that a certain amount of flexibility might be allowed when it comes to those included here, or in some cases, those which may have been missed out.

When war memorials were first decided upon and subsequently designed, built and unveiled, there was no officially approved criteria as to who should be named on a particular memorial or roll of honour. It was literarily down to those who came up with the idea and raised the money to pay for the memorial or roll of honour who then decided who should be named on them. This would differ from area to area.

Take for example Billericay in Essex. Billericay, Little Burstead, Great Burstead and Stock are all literarily a stone's throw away from each other. The latter three are still villages, whilst Billericay is a town which is part of the London commuter belt; yet they all sit within a couple of miles of each other. Each has its own war memorial and there are some men who are named on three out of the four. How that came about and why the men were claimed by more than one of the areas is not clear, but it once again highlights the confusion surrounding the issue.

Most towns and villages have churches which are festooned with rolls of honour, either dedicated to influential families, or groups of their parishioners who fell during the Great War or numerous other conflicts across the years. Most of these will also then be duplicated or even replicated more than once on nearby war memorials.

My apologies to anybody who feels that I may have got some wrong by either including or omitting them.

Darenth Hospital War Memorial

The Darenth Hospital War Memorial today sits in Darenth Country Park which was built on the site of Darenth Park and Mabledon Hospitals, for the treatment of patients with psychiatric problems. Both of the hospitals had cemeteries within their grounds. The war memorial was unveiled on 16 December 1927 by General Fell.

Over the years the hospital possessed different names, which were not exactly complimentary by today's standards. It started out life as the Metropolitan Imbecile Asylum – whoever chose that name did not want any confusion circulated about its purpose. By the time of the First World War it had changed its name, rather more subtly, to the Darenth Industrial Colony.

The memorial is dedicated to the hospital staff who were killed in both world wars. There are eleven names commemorated from the First World War.

Darenth Hospital War Memorial.

Ball, J.W.	Byrne, H.B.	Couchman, A.E.
Crowhurst, S.G.	Crowhurst, W.R.	Gladwell, J.
Harrington, T.J.	Holloway, W.A.	McNab, A.F.
Roberts, J.	Spensley, F.O.	

Here are some of those named on the memorial in more detail. Ideally I would have liked to include a piece about each one of them, but sometimes it just is not possible as the information is not available. For example, the first name on the Darenth Hospital War Memorial is **J.W. Ball**. A check on the CWGC website shows fourteen men with the same name and initials who fell during the First World War. One of them was a Joseph William Ball, a lance corporal in the 10th (Service) Battalion, Queen's Own (West Kent Regiment) who could be the same man.

He had married Rosetta Isabella Spells on 1 September 1913 at Erith in Kent. Their son Alfred William Ball, was born 18 June 1914 in Dartford. After the war Joseph's wife remarried, becoming Mrs Helliwell and was living at 27 Gayford Way, Crayford, Dartford, which is another indicator that it is the same person that is commemorated on the memorial.

Joseph's army service number was G/10682. When checked against his army service record, which has thankfully survived, this shows that he enlisted in the Regular Army, 10th Battalion, Queen's Own (Royal West Kent Regiment), at Maidstone on 6 November 1915. Prior to this he had been a private (20151) in the 2nd/5th Battalion, No.3 Support Company, Queen's Own (Royal West Kent Regiment), which was a Territorial Unit and from which he was discharged on 5 November 1915, thus allowing him to enlist in the Regular Army. At the time of his enlistment he was 29 years old and his home address was shown as 246 Lowfield Street, Dartford. It also showed that his 'trade or calling' was that of a baker.

Joseph had two younger brothers, Edward Albert and Alfred James Ball along with two sisters, Hilda Gertrude Ball and Rosa May, who was married and had the surname of Vince. In 1920, both of Joseph's parents, George and Anna Elizabeth Ball, were still alive.

Joseph arrived in France with his battalion on 4 May 1916 having sailed from Southampton the previous evening. The battalion had been raised on 3 May 1915 by Lord Harris, who at the time was the Vice

Lord Lieutenant of Kent. He had done so at the bequest of the Army Council.

Joseph was struck down with influenza on 3 November 1916 and had to be admitted to the 140th Field Ambulance where he stayed for two months, so bad was his condition. He was returned to duty on 4 January, only two weeks before he died of his wounds on 18 January 1917. He was buried at the Lijssenthoek Military Cemetery, which is situated at Poperinghe, in Belgium. The cemetery contains the graves of 9,901 Commonwealth servicemen who fell during the Great War. There are also a total of 883 French and German soldiers buried there, and is the second largest cemetery of Commonwealth servicemen in Belgium.

Frank Oswald Spensley was 39 years old and served in Salonika as a captain in the Royal Army Medical Corps. He died of pneumonia on 23 October 1918. He was a member of the Royal College of Surgeons and before the war had been the senior medical officer at the Darenth Industrial Colony.

His parents, the Rev James and Catherine Spensley, were from Reeth in Yorkshire but in the 1911 Census they are shown as living at 2 Dolphin Road, Slough, Berkshire, with James as a Wesleyan Methodist preacher, the change in location being connected to James's religious role.

Frank's elder siblings, Kent and Kate Spensley, were still living with their parents, although by now Kate has married and had a five-month-old son, also named Frank. I could find no record of Kent having served in the military during the war.

Albert Edward Couchman enlisted at Bromley and became a guardsman (21210) in No.4 Company, 3rd Battalion, Grenadier Guards. He arrived in France with his battalion on 26 July 1915 and was killed in action between 14 and 17 September 1916. He was 37 years of age. His body was never recovered so his name is commemorated on the Thiepval Memorial on the Somme.

Before the war he was a gas stoker working for the Metropolitan Asylum Board. His wife, Ellen Maud Couchman, lived at 14 Mount Pleasant Road, Dartford.

John Jeffery Gladwell worked in the 'mess' at the Darenth Industrial

Colony prior to enlisting in the army early in the war. He became a lance corporal (4794) in the 6th Battalion, Queen's Own (Royal West Kent Regiment) and died of his wounds on 12 April 1917. He was 36 years of age.

His parents, George and Ann Jeffery, lived at Southfleet, Gravesend and his wife, Amelia Emily Gladwell, lived at 5 Lincolnshire Terrace, Lanes End, Dartford.

S.G. Crowhurst was born on 1 January 1886 in Woolwich. He enlisted in the army on 6 April 1904, serving for seven years until 1911, when he joined the Army Reserve. He was called up on mobilization on 5 August 1914 as a lance corporal (7648) in the 1st Battalion, Queen's Own (Royal West Kent Regiment). The battalion landed at Le Havre on 15 August 1914, becoming some of the first troops to do so. They were involved in the war's first major battle at Mons on 23 August 1914, which was followed three days later by more bloody fighting at Le Cateau. In October that year the battalion made a heroic stand at the Battle of Neuve Chapelle which began on 10 March 1915. The fighting lasted for three days, at the end of which the 1st Battalion had lost 450 men out of a total of 750.

He subsequently died of his wounds received in action on the Western Front on 10 May 1917. He is buried at the Aubigny Communal Cemetery Extension, in the Pas de Calais region of France. It contains the graves of 2,771 Commonwealth servicemen from the First World

Aubigny Communal Cemetery Extension.

War. There are also 64 German soldiers as well as 227 French soldiers buried there from the same period.

The De Ruvigny's Roll of Honour, 1914-1919 has him recorded as S.T. Crowhurst, whereas the CWGC has him as S.G. Crowhurst

William Richard Crowhurst was born at Dartford in 1894. When war broke out he enlisted and became an acting bombardier (46445) in 'B' Battery, 106 Brigade, Royal Field Artillery. He arrived in France on 29 August 1915.

He was killed in action on 28 July 1917 aged 23 and is buried at the Perth Cemetery (China Wall) which is situated in Ypres, in Belgium. There are 2,791 Commonwealth servicemen buried in the cemetery, of which a staggering 1,369 are unidentified.

William's parents, Richard and Emily Crowhurst, lived in Kent, but prior to the war he had lived with his wife Edith, at 13 Trevelyan Street, Eccles, Manchester.

The 1911 Census showed the family living at 20 Powder Mill Lane, Wilmington, Dartford. William had two younger brothers, Ernest and William, neither of whom served in the war, as well as an elder sister, Edith.

Theodore Jack Harrington was a lance corporal (8798) in the 1st Battalion, Royal Irish Regiment, when he was killed in action on 2 June 1915. His army service record shows that he had enlisted on 21 November 1905 in London when he was a month away from his nineteenth birthday. He signed on for twelve years, three years with the colours and nine more in the reserve. The CWGC shows him as being 26 years of age when he was killed, which would mean that if they are correct, he would have only been 16 when he enlisted.

Besides serving in both France and Belgium, prior to the war he had also seen service with his regiment in India.

He has no known grave and is commemorated on the Ploegsteert Memorial to the Missing, south of Ypres in Belgium. Most of the 11,000 men who are commemorated on the memorial were killed in some of the war's major battles, but also in the course of routine day to day trench warfare which regularly took place in the area.

Theodore's parents, George and Marie Jane Harrington, lived at 17 Half Way Street, Sidcup, Kent.

W.A. Holliday was a private (G/35497) in the 10th (Royal East Kent and West Kent Yeomanry) Battalion, The Buffs (East Kent Regiment). He was killed in action just a month before the end of the war, on 10 October 1918. He is buried in the Rue-David Military Cemetery, at Fleurbaix.

Rue David Military Cemetery, Fleurbaix.

Swanscombe – St Peter & St Paul Church

The ornately carved wooden and glass roll of honour, sits proudly in the church of St Peter and St Paul in Swanscombe, Kent. It contains and commemorates the names of eighty-two young men from Swanscombe who lost their lives as a result of the First World War.

The centrepiece of the roll of honour contains the names of those who lost their lives in the First World War, whilst the outer two 'folding doors' contain the names of servicemen and civilians who were killed during the Second World War.

At the time of the First World War, Swanscombe had 1,556 homes and out of the hundreds of young men who went off to fight, 138 of them never came back, which meant that on average one out of every ten homes in the town suffered a bereavement. That does not of course include those who were wounded.

Swanscombe - St Peter & St Paul Church.

Here are the names of the fallen, some of whom I will look at in closer detail.

Arthur Ainsley
Archibald S. Aylward
Henry James Barden
Percy Bartholomew
John William Beatrup
Frederick James Bennett
William Bolton
Ernest Bridger
Joe Brown
Stanley Chandler
Richard Charles Cherry
Charles Clements
Percy James Cole
Percy Cooper
William Croucher

Henry George Danzey
Thomas Darge
John Henry Down
Alfred Embleton
James Charles Ellen
George Eyres
Alfred Victor Farmer
George Farmer
Henry George Flexon
Edward Valentine Freed
Ernest Freeman
John Giles
Ernest Walter Graves
Charles Goodwin
Walter Harding

Edward William Hardy
Edward Haylock
Charles Hazel
Arthur Hills
Joseph Hoadley
William Hoadley
Albert Edward Howard
Donald Humble
Robert James
Percy Frederick Jackson
Edwin King
Stanley Malyon
Herbert George Kitchener
Albert Edward Larner
Charles Edward Latter
Henry Thomas Loft
Herbert L.E. Ludlow
Frederick Malyon
James Mannering
George Mason
Charles Alfred Mason
William Matom
Frank Medhurst
Stewart William Mercer
John Messam
Louis Openshaw

Harry Outred
Leonard Outred
Harry Ovens
Charles William Palmer
Robert Perkins
John A. Wynard Peyton
John Randle
Ernest Edwin Phillips
Owen Thomas Poll
Benjamin Wood
Henry George Raven
Elvey Day
Henry William Raven
Oscar Salter Roberts
John Russell
Henry Alfred Simmons
John Henry Simmons
Arthur Edward South
Alfred Stone
Edwin Benjamin Stanley
Alfred Tickner
Frederick Tickner
Alfred John Tigwell
William Walter
John White

John William Beatrup is the name recorded on the St Peter and St Paul Church roll of honour, but the CWGC website shows his name as James William Beatrup. On the Ancestry.co.uk website under the section 'UK Soldiers Died in the Great War' it also shows the name James William Beatrup, as do the British Army First World War Medal Rolls Index Cards. The 1911 Census also shows James W. Beatrup living at 69 Knockhall Chase, Greenhithe, Swanscombe, Kent.

Whichever of the two names is correct he was a private (6390) (253053) in the 3rd (City of London) Battalion (Royal Fusiliers), London Regiment who was killed in action whilst serving on the Western Front on 24 March 1918.

If it is accepted that his name was in fact James and not John, then sadly his name has been incorrectly recorded on the church's roll of honour.

James Beatrup had two brothers, Frank who was born in 1886, and Percy, who was born in 1888. We can find no record of Frank having served in the military during the First World War although he lived until he was 65, and died at Chatham in 1951.

Percy served as a private (C/9340) in the King's Royal Rifle Corps and was awarded both the British War Medal and the Victory Medal. He survived the war, living until the age of seventy-seven, passing away at Dartford in 1965.

Harry Thomas Darge was a petty officer (210083) in the Royal Navy on board HMS *Russell* when he was killed on 27 April 1916 aged 32, by a mine explosion off Malta. He has no known grave and his name is commemorated on the Chatham Naval Memorial.

HMS *Russell* was a Duncan Class Royal Naval Battleship that was first launched in Hull in 1901. She had been attached to numerous 'fleets' and 'battle squadrons' before joining the Channel Fleet in November 1914. Later in the war in January 1916 she was involved in the evacuation of troops from the Gallipoli Peninsula.

When striking two sea mines off Malta on 27 April 1916, 126 of her crew were killed including Harry Thomas Darge, but a further 625 of the crew, which included the ship's admiral and captain, survived.

Ironically the ship had only arrived in Malta the day before she struck the mine just outside the Grand Harbour. The mines had been laid by the German submarine *U-73* which was under the command of Gustav Siess.

Harry's mother, Elizabeth Darge, lived at 87 Church Road, Swanscombe, Greenhithe, Kent.

Joseph Hoadley was a private (G/2286) in the 7th Battalion, Queen's Own (Royal West Kent Regiment). He was killed in action on 13 June 1916 and was the first of the two Hoadley sons to be killed in the war. He has no known grave and his name is commemorated on the Thiepval Memorial on the Somme.

Joseph and William's parents, George and Mary Hoadley, lived at 97 Milton Road, Swanscombe, Kent. Like many families during the war, they had to endure the sadness of losing not one but two sons in the fighting. They had to reconcile their loss with the knowledge that their bodies were never found and their names had been commemorated on separate war memorials on the other side of the English Channel.

William Hoadley was a private (G/6461) in the 1st Battalion, Queen's Own (Royal West Kent Regiment). He was killed in action on 9 April 1917, aged 36. He is commemorated on the Arras Memorial.

Henry Thomas Loft was a private (17675) in the 1st Battalion, East Surrey Regiment when he was killed on 31 August 1916 during the Battle of the Somme. He has no known grave and his name is commemorated on the Thiepval Memorial on the Somme. It is one of the most impressive memorials in France that keeps alive the names of those who were killed during the Battle of the Somme, but whose bodies were never recovered.

Thiepval Memorial. (Commonwealth War Graves Commission)

Charles Alfred Mason was a corporal (24271) in the Royal Army Veterinary Corps working at the 11th Veterinary Hospital. He died on 26 April 1919, aged 36. His wife Agnes lived at 19 Springfield Road, Northfleet, Kent.

Charles is buried in the Mikra British Cemetery in Kalamaria, Greece which was opened in April 1917, remaining in use for further burials until 1920. The cemetery was increased in size at the end of the war when the remains of other fallen soldiers were brought in from other nearby burial grounds. It now contains 1,810 Commonwealth graves from the First World War.

Harry Outred was a private (G/2296) in 'D' Company, 7th Battalion, Queen's Own (Royal West Kent Regiment), the same battalion as his younger brother Leonard. Harry was killed in action on 13 July 1916, less than two weeks into the Battle of the Somme. His body was never found and, like tens of thousands of other brave young men, it is commemorated on the Thiepval Memorial.

Leonard Outred was a private (G/12227) in the 7th Battalion, Queen's Own (Royal West Kent Regiment) when he was killed in action on 27 September 1916. He is buried in the Connaught Cemetery at Thiepval.

Connaught Cemetery, Thiepval. (Commonwealth War Graves Commission)

The 26th Reserve Division of the German Army held Thiepval and its surrounding areas when Commonwealth forces launched their attack on the area on 1 July 1916. It would not be an easy task by any stretch of the imagination; and so it proved to be, as it was not until 26 September 1916 that Thiepval finally fell. Even then the area was not entirely safe, as the very next day Leonard Outred was killed.

The war was one of mixed emotions for Harry and Leonard's parents, Alfred and Eliza Outred, who when the 1911 Census was taken, lived at 2 Bessie Villas, Milton Road, Swanscombe, Greenhithe, Kent. They had three other children, Ethel, Thomas and Alfred, both sons having also served in the war and survived. Of the four brothers only Leonard's army service record has not survived.

Alfred Outred, the eldest of the brothers, attested at Maidstone on 14 February 1916 when he was 36 years old. It would be exactly ten months before he was actually called up, on 14 December 1916, at Gravesend, by which time his brothers Harry and Leonard had been killed in the fighting. He also became a private (G/23443) in the Queen's Own (Royal West Kent Regiment), remained in the army until well after the war had finished, not being transferred to the Army Reserve until 16 October 1919.

Thomas Outred was the first of the brothers to join up, enlisting only a month in to the war on 7 September 1914 at Maidstone, when he also became a private (G/2283) in the Queen's Own (Royal West Kent Regiment). He was officially demobbed from the army at Hounslow on 18 February 1919. Thomas did not survive the war entirely unscathed as he had received a gunshot to the chest, which left him with pulmonary tuberculosis. For his injuries he was awarded a war pension of 40s a week, which only lasted for fourteen months. It would appear that he was wounded during the early days of the Battle of the Somme as he arrived back in the UK on 6 July 1916 having been in France since 26 July 1915. After spending time in hospital recuperating from his wounds, he returned to France on 3 March 1917 where he remained until 25 June 1918 when he was given two weeks home leave. He returned to France for a third time on 9 July 1918 where he stayed for a month before returning home on 26 August 1918. His war was over at last.

By the time Thomas had received his 1914-15 Star, British War and

Victory Medal's on 16 July 1921, he was living at 65 Church Road in Swanscombe.

Henry George Danzey was a private (S/9206) in the 6th Battalion, Queen's Own (Royal West Kent Regiment) when he was killed in action on 3 July 1916, just three days into the Battle of the Somme. His body was never found so he has no known grave, but his name is commemorated on the Thiepval Memorial.

Henry George Flexon was an air mechanic 2nd class (146843) in the 53rd Wing, Royal Air Force when he died of pneumonia on 28 February 1919; he was only 19 years of age and is buried at Swanscombe Cemetery in Kent. His parents, Stephen and Mary Flexon, lived at 39 Knockhall Road, in Greenhithe.

Herbert George Kitchener, who was no relation to the more illustrious Lord Kitchener, was a private (63623) in the 13th Battalion, Royal Fusiliers when he died of his wounds on 2 April 1918. He was 25 years old and was laid to rest at the Doullens Communal Cemetery Extension No.1. There are some 1,335 Commonwealth soldiers buried there, as well as a further 374 who are buried in the No.2 extension.

Doullens was the headquarters of the French military leader Marshall Foch early in the war, as well as the location for the conference in March 1918 which led to his becoming the commander of the Allied armies on the Western Front.

The main medical unit in the area between the beginning of 1917 and June 1918 was the 3rd Canadian Stationary Hospital which is where Herbert would have had his wounds treated.

His parents, George and Annie Kitchener, lived at 111 High Street, East Ham, London.

John William Messam was a private (CH/16830) in the Royal Marine Light Infantry, attached to HMS *Pathfinder* when he was killed just one month into the war on 5 September 1914.

HMS *Pathfinder* was a Pathfinder class of Scout Cruiser. She also holds the distinction, if that's the right word to use, of having been the first ship to be sunk by a locomotive torpedo fired by a submarine. She was built by Cammell Laird shipbuilders in Birkenhead, launched on 16 July 1904 and commissioned a year later on 18 July 1905. By the outbreak of the First World War she was part of the 8th Destroyer Flotilla which was based at Rosyth in the Firth of Forth.

The *Pathfinder* was sunk off St Abbs Head, Berwickshire, which is on the North East coast, by the German U-Boat *U-21* under the command of Kapitanleutnant Otto Hersing. It was his first victory.

One of the big disadvantages that Scout Cruisers had was that their engines were coal fed, which meant that the maximum speeds they could reach were not much better than about 5 knots making them easy targets, this was the case with HMS *Pathfinder*. She was struck in one of her magazines which exploded, resulting in her sinking within a matter of minutes, taking 259 of the crew, including John Messam, to a watery grave. His name is commemorated on the Naval Memorial at Chatham.

Charles William Palmer was a private (T/202506) in the 1st Battalion, The Buffs (East Kent Regiment) when he was killed in action on 21 March 1918. His name is commemorated on the Arras War Memorial as he has no known grave. His father, Thomas Palmer, lived at 3 Swanscombe Street, Swanscombe, Kent.

John Algernon Wynyard Peyton was a lieutenant in the 7th Battalion, Norfolk Regiment. He was killed in action on 22 August 1918 at the age of 25. He is buried at the Ribemont Communal Cemetery Extension, on the Somme.

The extension part of the cemetery was begun in May 1918 and used until August 1918, during which time sixty-eight burials took place, carried out by units who were engaged in the defence of Amiens. After the signing of the Armistice, the remains of soldiers who had initially been buried in other nearby cemeteries were exhumed and re-buried in the Ribemont Extension Cemetery. His parents, Captain F.H. Peyton RN and Helen Peyton, lived at 'Westcroft', Gravesend, Kent.

Henry Alfred Simmons was a private (253055) in the 1st/3rd Battalion, London Regiment (Royal Fusiliers). He was just 20 years old when he was killed in action on 15 August 1917. His body was never found but his name is commemorated on the Ypres (Menin Gate) War Memorial. His parents lived at 99 Knockhall Road, Greenhithe, Kent.

Ribemont Extension Cemetery. (Commonwealth War Graves Commission)

Alfred Tickner was a gunner (41657) in the Royal Field Artillery. He enlisted at Woolwich on 30 January 1906 after having previously served with the 3rd Battalion, West Kent Regiment, which was a local militia.

He married a local girl, Lily Frances Baker, who also lived in Swanscombe, on 7 June 1913 at the Registry Office in Dartford and their address, which was recorded on Alfred's attestation form, was 30 Swanscombe Street, Swanscombe, Kent. His parents lived at 46 Sun Road, Swanscombe.

At the outbreak of the war his unit was in Scotland and was mobilized on 5 August 1914, within hours of war with Germany having being declared. It arrived in France two weeks later on 18 August. Alfred died of his wounds on 1 October 1917.

The 1911 Census shows Frederick Tickner was born in Swanscombe in 1891, and like his elder brother Alfred, was already serving in the army. He was in the 2nd Battalion, Royal West Kent Regiment, stationed in India.

Alfred John Tigwell was a private (78020) in the Royal Army Medical Corps who was killed on 2 April 1918. He is buried in the Hangard Communal Cemetery Extension on the Somme.

Hangard Communal Cemetery Extension.

At the end of March 1918 Hangard was part of the area that was being defended by Allied forces defending Amiens and was the scene of some vicious and incessant fighting, it was during this conflict that Alfred was killed.

As the extension to the Communal Cemetery at Hangard wasn't opened until August 1918, it is more than likely that Alfred was initially buried elsewhere and his body exhumed and moved to Hangard after the Armistice. There were at least thirteen smaller cemeteries in the immediate area around Hangard.

Swanscombe – All Saints Church

THESE ALL GAVE THEIR LIVES 1914-1918
JOHN ANDERSON : RICHARD BAKER : PERCY BARDEN
HENRY BARDEN : LEONARD BARDOE : CYRIL BARE
WILLIAM BARE : WALTER BAREHAM : GEORGE C BERRIMAN
JOHN BOBBY : HERBERT C BOBBY : WILLIAM BONES
WILFRED S. BOWEN : SAMUEL BRIGHT : EDWARD BROAD
THOMAS BROAD : CHARLES N BROAD : ROBERT A BUTCHARD
ERNEST CLARK : GEORGE CRUST : HENRY DALTRY
HENRY J. DUNMALL : FRED G. ELLEN : CHARLES W. FINCH
ROBERT FLINT : HAROLD FOREMAN : THOMAS GODDEN
HENRY GRAY : ROBERT GREEN : STEPHEN R. GROOMBRIDGE
JOHN GURR : FRED HUDSON : THOMAS JARVIS
HAROLD JESSUP : WILLIAM LOFT : HUBERT MARTIN
STEWART W. MERCER : HERBERT E. NEWDICK : HARRY OVENS
JAMES T. PIPER : WILLIAM PLUMMER : OWEN E. POLL
FRED PRICE : HENRY ROBINSON : FRANK ROBINSON
GEORGE SEADEN : NELSON SKEWS : PERCY SMITH
ALFRED SMITH : LOUIS STEVENS : HARRY STONEHAM
WILLIAM SULLIVAN : JOHN TUCKER : GEORGE TURNER
WILLIAM TURNER : GEORGE WEBSTER : HARRY WELLAR
GEORGE WHITE : JOHN WHITE : ARTHUR WOODGER
GLORY·TO·GOD·WHO·GAVE·STRENGTH·TO·ENDURE

Swanscombe - All Saints Church.

There are the names of sixty-one young men from the All Saints parish who paid the ultimate price during the First World War, recorded on the church's roll of honour. As a mark of respect their names are now cherished and not forgotten by those who have followed them.

The world changed dramatically after the First World War, most of it an improvement on what had gone before. There were social and economic changes that quite possibly wouldn't have come along if it had not been for the war: pensions for the elderly, the right to vote for both men and women, the latter gradually becoming more and more integrated into the working environment. Society had changed forever and there was no going back to yesteryear. In the war, the common man had fought and died alongside the aristocracy and the landed gentry; when peace came he wanted and expected more out of life.

Here are the names of those brave young men who paid the ultimate price for a better tomorrow.

John Anderson
Richard Baker
Percy Barden
Henry Barden
Leonard Bardoe
Cyril Bare
William Bare
Walter Bareham
George C. Berriman
John Bobby
Henry C. Bobby
William Bones
William Bones
Wilfred S. Bowen
Samuel Bright
Edward Broad
Thomas Broad
Charles N. Broad
Robert A. Butchard
Ernest Clark
George Crust
Henry Dalton
Henry J. Dunmall
Fred G. Ellen
Charles W. Finch
Robert Flint
Harold Foreman
Thomas Gooden
Henry Gray
Robert Green
John Gurr

Stephen Groombridge
Fred Hudson
Thomas Jarvis
Harold Jessup
William Loft
Hubert Martin
Stewart W. Mercer
Herbert Newdick
Harry Owens
James J. Piper
William Plummer
Owen E. Poll
Fred Price
Henry Robinson
Frank Robinson
George Seaden
Nelson Skews
Percy Smith
Alfred Smith
Louis Stevens
Harry Stoneham
William Sullivan
John Tucker
George Turner
William Turner
George Webster
Harry Wellar
George White
John White
Arthur Woodger

Let's take a look at a few of the above names in a bit more detail.

Lance Corporal Percy Barden (G/2287) was in the 7th Battalion, Queen's Own (Royal West Kent Regiment). The Battle of the Somme was less than two weeks old when Percy was killed in action on 13 July 1916.

The Allied offensive had begun on 1 July and had been preceded by a week long artillery bombardment of the German defensive positions. The expectation by Allied commanders was that in the aftermath of the onslaught, victory was almost a foregone conclusion. How wrong that assumption would turn out to be was going to be hammered home in the costliest way possible. On the first day alone the losses were catastrophic with Commonwealth forces having suffered almost 60,000 casualties, 20,000 of whom were killed.

One of the original objectives for the attack was the village of Thiepval. It would be another three months before it was taken. Percy has no known grave and is one of the 70,000 names that are commemorated on the Thiepval Memorial to the missing.

Rifleman (C/9719) Leonard George Bardoe was with the 20th Battalion, King's Royal Rifle Corps and also involved in the fighting at the Battle of the Somme. He died the day after Percy was killed, on 14 July 1916.

There was a certain irony attached to their lives as well as their deaths. Here were two young men who were not only from the same village and attended the same church, but had probably attended the same school. When the call to arms came they both joined up to fight for king and country. Although in different regiments, they both fought in the Battle of the Somme and both were killed. Whether either of them knew that the other was there is not known. Their names appear above one another on the roll of honour at All Saints Church in Swanscombe and they are both commemorated on the Thiepval Memorial.

George Charles Berriman was a very interesting character. He had been born at Fort Muchiborne in the province of Bengal in India in 1878, indicating that his father had been a military man as well.

Although we are not exactly sure when, George had previously served for eight years as a gunner (2673), but it is known that he was involved in the Second Boer War (1899 – 1902) as he was awarded the South Africa Medal with the Queen's Clasp. The best estimate is that it would have been from about 1900 to 1908 at which time, having served the eight years that he had signed up for, he was transferred on to the Army Reserve.

George enlisted for the second time at Gravesend on 10 November 1914 at the age of 36 and once again became a gunner (2534) in the Royal Garrison Artillery. He was promoted to the rank of bombardier on 2 August 1916, but less than six months later on 9 February 1917 he was discharged from the army as no longer fit enough for war service, with no explanation as to what was actually wrong with him.

He had married Marion Agnes Stoddard in Edinburgh 2 December 1907. They had three children, two sons and a daughter. George was their eldest, born in May 1909. James followed in January 1912 and finally Marion, who was born in June 1914, seven weeks before the outbreak of the war.

According to the 1911 Census the family home was at 10 Stanhope Road, Swanscombe, Greenhithe, Kent and George's occupation was shown as a 'Cement Cook Filler', but what that actually entailed, it is not possible to be sure.

He died at home in December 1918 and, as he is included in the church's roll of honour, it can only be surmised that his death was linked to his time in the military and the reason why he was eventually discharged from the army.

Herbert Edwin Newdick was from Tuddenham, Suffolk but had for many years lived in Swanscombe with his wife Rosina. They married in Dartford on 8 August 1897 and had three children: Rosina, who was born in 1899, Frederick who was born in 1901 and Anne who was born in 1912.

A Petty Officer 1st Class (129475) in the Royal Navy, he was killed at the age of 49 on 15 October 1917 when the ship he was on board, the MFA *Whitehead*, a steamer built in 1880, was torpedoed and sunk by the German submarine, *UC-74* some 40 miles north of Suda Bay, Crete.

There are differing reports in relation to the actual casualty numbers sustained by the *Whitehead*. Some state that twenty-three of the crew were killed, whilst other reports break this down into fifteen of the crew killed, with another eight having been picked up and taken prisoner by *UC-74*. The latter report comes from the war diaries of *UC-74*. A further twelve crew members were picked up by the destroyer *Renard*.

Herbert's body was never recovered. His name is commemorated on the Chatham Naval Memorial. His wife Rosina died in 1954 at the age of seventy-six.

Lieutenant Robert Archibald Butchard of the 31st Battalion, Royal Fusiliers was 23 years old when he was killed in action during fighting between Les Boeufs and Gueudecourt in France on 5 November 1916. He is buried in the Guards Cemetery at Lesboeufs. His father, George William Butchard, lived at Grove House, Northfleet, Gravesend, Kent.

Private Nelson Skews (G/1586), 10th Battalion, Queen's Own (Royal West Kent Regiment), died on 19 January 1919. He is buried at the Cologne Southern Cemetery in Germany along with more than 1,000 other Allied prisoners of war. More than 300,000 Commonwealth soldiers were captured during the war and 12,000 of them died in captivity as a result of wounds, ill treatment and disease.

Arthur Woodger was a private (G/12134) in the 7th Battalion, Queen's Own (Royal West Kent Regiment). He was 28 years old when he was killed on 3 May 1917. He has no known grave and his name is commemorated on the Arras Memorial which records the names of some 35,000 Allied servicemen who died between the spring of 1916 and August 1918.

Arthur's parents lived at 63 High Street, Galley Hill, Swanscombe, Kent.

Private Henry J. Dunmall (187), 6th Battalion, Queen's Own (Royal West Kent Regiment) died on 26 October 1916. His parents, George and Sarah Dunmall, lived in Swanscombe.

He is buried at the Étaples Military Cemetery in the Pas de Calais, which is the final resting place for 10,771 Commonwealth servicemen. The large number of burials must be looked at in the context of the many hospitals that were in the area throughout the war, where unfortunately not all recovered from their wounds.

During the First World War the area of Étaples, near to the French coast, was a major staging post both for fresh troops waiting to 'go up the line', as well as a large medical centre with numerous hospitals to deal with the wounded troops that were continually coming in from the fighting further inland. The medical facilities included many different types of hospitals, ranging from general ones, Red Cross hospitals as well as a large convalescent area. Collectively they had the capacity to deal with 22,000 wounded and sick soldiers.

In one period during 1917 it has been estimated that there were in excess of 100,000 Commonwealth and Allied troops in the Étaples area. There were still three of the hospitals and the convalescent centre, operating in the area as late as September 1919, some ten months after the end of the war. Its location was remote from attack and readily accessible by rail from both the north and south of France.

John Henry Gurr aged 34, was a ship's corporal 1st Class (190332), Royal Navy, serving on board HMS *Cressy* when, just seven weeks into the war, he was killed in action on 22 September 1914.

HMS *Cressy* was an armoured cruiser which was launched on 4 December 1899 in the Govan shipyards in Scotland. Prior to the war she had seen service in both North America and the West Indies and soon after the start of the First World War she became part of the 7th Cruiser Squadron, which was tasked with patrolling the North Sea to prevent German warships from attempting to attack the supply route between England and France, which including both cargo vessels as well as troop carriers.

HMS *Cressy* took part in the very first naval battle of the war on 28 August 1914 – the Battle of Heligoland Bight – when ships from the Royal Navy attacked German destroyers in the North Sea off the north-west coast of Germany.

A British fleet, numbering some forty-six vessels and including destroyers, light cruisers, submarines, as well as five battle cruisers, were commanded by Vice Admiral David Beatty. In the ensuing battle, which was a clear victory for the British, only four of their ships were damaged but none were sunk. They suffered seventy-five casualties, which included thirty-five killed. When put in context to German losses it was clear just how one sided an affair this battle actually was. Four of their ships were sunk, a further three were damaged. They lost 712 men who were killed, 530 who were injured and a further 336 who were taken prisoner by the British.

After the battle *Cressy* had to ferry 165 captured German prisoners of war back to mainland Britain.

It was a different story a few weeks later on the morning of 22 September 1914, however. HMS *Cressy* was on patrol alongside her

HMS Cressy. *(Wikipedia)*

sister ships, HMS *Aboukir* and HMS *Hogue*. Unbeknown to the three ships, the German submarine *U-9*, commanded by Kapitanleutnant Otto Weddigen, was submerged nearby having been earlier forced to dive to avoid an early morning storm. When she eventually surfaced she came across the three British ships. He wasted no time in utilising his sudden and unexpected advantage, firing his first torpedo at 0620, striking *Aboukir* on her starboard side. Not surprisingly confusion and surprise were now the main controlling factors, with it initially assumed that the *Aboukir* had struck a mine.

The *Hogue* and *Cressy* approached their stricken sister ship to pick up survivors. The *Aboukir* was now a sitting duck; she was listing badly and was literally dead in the water. By now *Hogue* was in close attendance and in an effort to pick up survivors had lowered her boats, when she was struck by two more torpedoes fired by *U-9*. Twenty minutes after being struck she had capsized and sunk.

Despite her gallant efforts to ram the submarine, *Cressy* failed and soon afterwards she too was struck by a torpedo and sank.

From all three ships combined, a total of 1,397 men and 62 officers were killed in the attack, 560 of these were from HMS *Cressy*. In total 837 men were rescued and saved from a icy grave in what undoubtedly would have been freezing cold water.

John Gurr's parents lived at Galley Hill Road, Norfleet, Kent whilst his wife Eva, lived at 14 Melbourne Road, Chatham. He is commemorated on the Naval War Memorial in Chatham.

Stephen Robert Groombridge was a private (MS/197) in the 61st Auxiliary Petrol Company, Mechanical Transport, Royal Army Service Corps, when he died of bronchial pneumonia on 16 February 1919 aged 36. He is buried at the Les Baraques Military Cemetery, Sangatte, in the Pas de Calais.

His parents, Henry and Ellen Groombridge, lived at Strood in Kent, whilst his wife, Emma Sarah Groombridge, lived at 16 Brighton Buildings, Tower Bridge Road, Bermondsey, London.

Harold Jessup enlisted in the army well before the war had even begun, on 24 January 1913 at Chatham, when he became a private (L/10332) in the 1st Battalion, Queen's (Royal West Surrey) Regiment.

He was killed in action on 31 October 1914 whilst serving on the

Perth Cemetery. (China Wall)

Western Front. He is buried in the oddly named Perth Cemetery (China War) in Ypres, Belgium. The reason for the confusing names is easily explained. Perth Cemetery is because soldiers from the 2nd Battalion, the Scottish Rifles helped in its building from June 1917 onwards, and most of the predecessors of the battalion were raised in Perth, Scotland. The China Wall connection came about from the nearby communication trench known as the Great Wall of China.

The cemetery was originally begun by French soldiers in November 1914. There are 2,791 Commonwealth servicemen who are buried there from the First World War, a staggering 1,369 of whom are unidentified.

Wilmington – War Memorial

The Wilmington War Memorial is located in the grounds of the village's primary school. There are thirty-eight names on the memorial which has been laid out in the year that each man died. As well as the man's surname and initials there is also the additional piece of information of his regiment.

The monument is wall mounted, made of stone with the individual names inscribed in two carved recesses in the shape of lancet windows.

The inscription on the memorial reads as follows:

Greater love hath no man than this. In memory of the men of Wilmington who gave their lives for their country 1914 – 1918.

Wilmington War Memorial.

1914

G. Broad (Buffs)

L. Bristow (RWK)

1915

W. Sparkes (Buffs)
T. Brown (RWK)
J. Crawley (CC)

H. Rawlings (ASC)
S. Wright (RFA)
F. Luck (24th Can)

1916

J. Rickwood (RFA)
H. Lynn (10th Husrs)
A. Johnson (RHA)
C. Letchford (RB)
F. Bolton (RWK)
C. Smith (RN)

H. Rose (RFA)
A. Couchman (RIR)
H. Bevens (RIR)
L.B. Wood (RB)
J.H. Rickwood (RFA)

1917

Couchman (Aux Fcs)
J. Symons (RN)
E. Roberts (RN)
A. Talbot (RB)
J. Mayger (RWK)

D. Crawley (C of L)
J. Casselton (RN)
Fry (10th Welsh)
W. Buggs (RB)

1918

G.T. Filmer (RWK)
C.G. Hobden (1st Northants)
C.W.E. Whitehead (Lt. RFC)
J.H. Golding (RR)
E. Garner (ASC)

W. Perryman MM (RAMC)
J. Wright (Buffs)
A. Stevens (Buffs)
G. Winch (RM)

1919

J.H.E. Whitehead

The first person from Wilmington to be killed in the war was **Private George Alfred Broad**. He was born in Wrotham, Kent, lived in Wilmington before the war and enlisted at Woolwich, as a private

(L/7751) in the 1st Battalion, Buffs, (East Kent Regiment). He was killed in action on 18 October 1914, with the war only ten weeks old, and has no known grave. His name is commemorated on the Ploegsteert Memorial to the Missing in Comines-Warneton, Belguim.

The date of George's death is significant as it saw the end of attempts by both sides at outflanking each other, as it was no longer possible

Ploegsteert War Memorial. (Commonwealth War Graves Commission)

after the fighting reached the sector of the Lys River. Between 9 and 18 October 1914 British casualties had reached 4,500.

George was a married man. His wife, Ann Norah Broad, was still living at 165 Daffodil Road, East Wickham, Welling, Kent after the war.

Private William Sparkes (79511), 2nd Battalion, The Buffs (East Kent Regiment) was killed on 11 February 1915, during fighting in the area of Zillebeke, south-east of Ypres. He was 20 years of age, has no known grave and his name is commemorated on the Ypres (Menin Gate) Memorial. His mother lived at 10 Main Road, Hextable, Kent.

At the outbreak of the war the 2nd Battalion was in Madras in India and returned to England, docking at Plymouth on 23 December 1914. They eventually arrived in France on 17 January 1915 where they remained until November of that year, before moving on to Salonika, where they remained for the rest of the war.

Stoker 1st Class Charles Frederick Smith lived at 26 Broad Lane, Wilmington, Kent, according to the 1911 Census. His parents were William and Annie Smith, his younger brothers, Albert (9) and Percy (2) and his sister, Beatrice (6). He was 14 years of age, had already left school and was working as a laundry hand in a warehouse.

Like most young men of his era, when the opportunity came to join up and do their bit, he did so willingly. For him it was to be life on the ocean wave, so he joined the Royal Navy and became a Stoker 1st Class (K/23109) serving on board HMS *Foxhound*, a torpedo boat destroyer. The ship was involved in the landings of British troops, (4th Battalion, Northamptonshire Regiment) at Suvla Bay at Gallipoli.

On Sunday, 8 October 1916 HMS *Foxhound* was at Salamis harbour, on the east coast of Cyprus at the mouth of the river Pedieos, just north of Famagusta, with other Allied forces who were there to try and bring Greece into the war on their side. The very next day, Stoker 1st Class

Capuccini Naval Cemetery, Malta.

Charles Frederick Smith died of an unknown illness. He is buried in Capuccini Naval Cemetery, Malta.

Private Albert Ernest Couchman (8315), 6th Battalion, Royal Irish Rifles was only 20 years of age when he was killed in action on 3 September 1916. He has no known grave and his name is commemorated on the Thiepval Memorial on the Somme. His parents lived at 14 Hook Green, Wilmington, Dartford.

The 6th Battalion were part of the 16th Division which was involved in the Battle of Guillemont between 3 and 6 September 1916, part of the Battle of the Somme.

Stoker 1st Class Ernest Roberts, Royal Navy, (K/21868) was serving on board the battleship HMS *Vanguard* when he died on Monday, 9 July 1917.

Just before midnight, HMS *Vanguard* was moored in the harbour at her base at Scapa Flow when a sudden and catastrophic explosion occurred. The ship sank, taking over 800 of her crew with her; only two crew members survived.

There has never been a definitive confirmation of exactly what happened that day, and different theories have been espoused over the years. The most likely is that the ship blew up due to an undetected fire which detonated cordite, which was used on board for firing the ship's guns

HMS Vanguard. *(Wikipedia)*

Staff Sergeant William Charles Perryman MM (534005), 4th (London) Field Ambulance, Royal Army Medical Corps, enlisted enlisted at Dartford. He died of his wounds on 20 April 1918 and is buried in the St Sever Cemetery Extension at Rouen.

His widow, Catherine Florence Perryman, was still living at 83 Hawley Road, Wilmington, Dartford after the war with their daughter, Elsie, who was eight years of age.

The war showed no grace or favour when it came to those who should die and those who would ultimately survive. It didn't know anything about wealth or place in society, it respected neither. Nowhere was that more cruelly shown than for the family of Sir George Hugh and Lady Gertrude Grace Whitehead, who during the First World War were living at Wilmington Hall, Wilmington near Dartford. They had two sons and three daughters as well as seven servants to look after them all. The war would sadly end up claiming both of their sons.

Out of the thirty-eight local men who fell during the First World War, they were two of the last from the village to be lost, with James actually being the last in 1919.

Lieutenant George William Edendale Whitehead, 53 Squadron Royal Air Force, was killed in action on 17 October 1918. No. 53 Squadron was formed at Catterick, North Yorkshire on 15 May 1916. It was originally intended to be just a training squadron but it was sent out to France in December that year to be used for reconnaissance purposes, originally with BE2e aircraft which were changed to RE8s in April 1917.

Harlebeke New British Cemetery. (Commonwealth War Graves Commission)

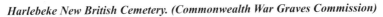

The squadron eventually returned to the UK in March 1919 to Old Sarum in Salisbury and was disbanded on 25 October 1919.

George is buried at the Harlebeke New British Cemetery in Belgium. Harlebeke village was not finally wrested from German control until the night of the 19-20 October 1918 by the 9th (Scottish) Division and the cemetery did not come in to existence until after the end of the war, which means that George was initially buried somewhere else and his remains moved to Harlebeke at a later time.

Second Lieutenant James Hugh Edendale Whitehead, 9th Battalion, Queen's Own (Royal West Kent Regiment), died of an unspecified sickness contracted whilst on active service, on 13 March 1919. He is buried in the family vault in St Michael and All Angels churchyard in Wilmington.

After the war Sir George and Lady Whitehead, moved to The Shrubbery, 72 Woodstock Road, Oxford.

The memorial shows there are two men with the surname of Rickwood who died during the war in 1916. They were brothers **Joseph Rickwood** and **James Henry Rickwood**, who in the 1901 Census are shown living with their parents, Joseph and Emma Rickwood, at Weeks Cottage, Charlton, Greenwich along with their one-year-old sister, Alice.

After this matters become slightly confusing depending on which record is correct, but the research shows that the two men were brothers and that their parents were Joseph and Emma Rickwood.

By the time of the 1911 Census, both Joseph and James Henry Rickwood had left home and joined the Army. Alice was still at home along with her brother Frederick, who was only six years of age, and the family were living at Hook Green, Stills Farm, Wilmington.

Joseph and James Henry both enlisted in the 82nd Battery, Royal Horse Artillery and Royal Field Artillery as Drivers, Joseph has the service number 63042 and James Henry has 75453.

On Ancestry.co.uk James Henry is shown as having died on 19 April 1916 while the CWGC gives his date of death as 29 April 1916. There is more confusion, as Ancestry.co.uk shows him as having died in Turkey whilst the CWGC shows him as having no known grave with his name being commemorated on the Basra War Memorial, in what is today's Iraq. This is slightly confusing, especially when he died in captivity as a prisoner of war, which would go some way to explaining the puzzle surrounding his date of death.

Joseph Rickwood died on 13 April 1916 in Egypt, not as a result of a bullet or a bomb, but because he had contracted malaria. This is once again slightly confusing as he is shown as having been buried in the Kut War Cemetery in Iraq.

The Rickwood brothers are a very good example of just how difficult it can be sometimes for writers of military history to get their facts absolutely correct, no matter how many sources they sift through to try and establish the truth.

Longfield – St Mary Magdalene Church

Longfield is a village in the Borough of Dartford and has had a church in the parish since 1343 making it over 750 years old. Part of it was extended slightly in the 1890s, although there is also evidence to suggest that there has been a place of worship on the same site dating back to the mid twelfth century.

The memorial is a small rough-hewn Celtic style wheel cross which sits on a square plinth and has a single step base. The inscription on it reads as follows:

'To the Glory of God 1914-1918/1939-1945 remember these your Brethren who passed out of sight by the path of duty and self-sacrifice giving their lives that others might live in freedom.'

The memorial contains the names of thirty-three young men from the parish who fell during the Great War.

H.J. Marchant	R. Stanley
E. Maples	W. Thompson
A. Munday	A. Wells
A. Oliver	T. Young
W. Oliver	J. Tomein
G. Peacock	L.T. Ashdown
R. Pankhurst	B.M. Adams
W. Pankhurst	E. Blackman
R. Rich	L. Beer
J. Simes	S. Burton
H. Swan	B. Caller

F. Cherry	R.D. Harrison
S. Day	D. Holmes
H. Day	A. Ing
W. Fothergill	R. Lynds
C. Foster	E. Martin
W Hoadley	

Here are more details on a few of the names:

According to the 1911 Census Henry and Bertha Pankhurst lived at 2 Kent Villas, Kent Road, Longfield, Kent with their daughter Louisa and six sons. Henry was the eldest of the sons at 28, then came Edwin, Archie, Benjamin, Frank and Ronald, who was the youngest aged 12.

I could find no records of either Benjamin or Frank having served during the First World War, but if they did it is certain that they both survived as Benjamin died in 1965 at the age of seventy-six and Frank died ten years later in 1975, aged eighty-three. Henry, Edwin and Archie all served during the war and survived.

Henry Pankhurst, who was a married man, enlisted at the age of 33 on 11 December 1915 at Maidstone and became a Private (40140) with the 8th Battalion, Lincolnshire Regiment. He served in France between 2 August 1916 and 3 November 1916. His return to England would appear to have come about as a result of spraining his ankle on 28 October 1916, so badly that he had to be admitted to the 2nd Australian General Hospital. On his return to England he was transferred to different units including the 258th Infantry Battalion, 51st Battalion, Durham Light Infantry and the 545th and 421st Agricultural Company, Labour Corps. He was demobilized on 6 September 1919. He was awarded a military pension, in part because he had acquired varicose veins, which were so bad that he spent eighty-one days as a patient at The Lord Derby War Hospital in Warrington, between 20 May 1919 and 8 August 1919. He died in 1974 aged 90.

Edwin Thomas Pankhurst enlisted on 5 February 1916 at Maidstone, becoming a private (59769) in the 33rd Labour Company, Royal Fusiliers, although his Attestation form shows that he joined from the Army Reserve, meaning that he had previously served in the army. He went on to serve in France from 2 April 1916 to 17 July 1918. Six weeks after his return he was discharged from the army as no longer physically fit for war service and awarded a silver badge, which indicates that the reason why he was discharged from the army was because he had been wounded. He died in 1960 aged 74.

Archie initially enlisted with the Duke of Cambridge's Own (Middlesex) Regiment where he was a private (12853) and later transferred to the Labour Corps as a private (3561972).

Private Ronald James Pankhurst (10282) enlisted at Gravesend initially in the Queen's Own (West Kent Regiment) before later transferring to 'D' Company 7th/8th Battalion, King's Own Scottish Borderers (242209). He died of his wounds on 13 June 1918 and is buried at the Aubigny Communal Cemetery Extension, in the Pas de Calais. There are 2,771 Commonwealth burials in the cemetery along with 227 French, as well as 64 German graves.

Although it must have been very sad for Henry and Emma Pankhurst to have lost Ronald to the war, there must have been a sense of relief to have had their other three sons survive it.

Sapper Edward Henry Blackman (2600), 1st/3rd Field Company, Royal Engineers was killed in action on 28 October 1915. He has no known grave and he is commemorated on the Helles War Memorial in Turkey which has the names of 21,000 Commonwealth soldiers inscribed on it.

Edward had two older brothers: Albert, who was born in 1888, and James who was born in 1889, neither of whom I could find anything definitive enough to show that they served during the First World War. Their parents, George and Mary Blackman, lived at 'Hollybush' Longfield Hill, Kent.

Private Private Reginald Walter Lynds (G/24508) enlisted at Gravesend and joined the 7th Battalion, Queen's Own (Royal West Kent Regiment). He was killed in action on 24 April 1918.

The 7th Battalion was raised in Maidstone on 5 September 1914 as part of Kitchener's Second New Army. After their initial training they left for France, arriving at Le Havre on 27 July 1915. In 1916 they saw action at the Battles of the Somme – Albert, Bazentin Ridge, Trônes Wood, Delville Wood, Thiepval, Ancre Heights, and Ancre. Throughout 1917 they were involved in more fighting at Miraumont, Irles, the German retreat to the Hindenberg Line, and the Third Battle of the Scarpe, the battles of Pilckem Ridge, Langemark, and the First and Second Battles of Passchendaele. During 1918 they continued in the thick of things at the Battles of St Quentin, Avre, Villers-Brettoneux, Amiens, Albert, the Second Battle of Bapaume, the Battle of Épehy, St Quentin Canal, Elle and lastly at the Sambre.

His name is commemorated on the Pozières Memorial which is situated on the Somme. The memorial commemorates over 14,000 servicemen from the United Kingdom and South Africa who have no known grave and who were killed on the Somme between 21 March and 7 August 1918.

His mother, Susanne Lynds, lived at Shipley Cottages, Longfield Hill, Dartford.

Fawkham War Memorial

The lettering on the granite plinth reads:
> *This cross is placed here in order that we may never forget*
> *Lt. Col. W.V. Dickinson CMG*
> *Lt. Col. H.R. Beddoes*
> *C. Haygreen E. Haygreen*
> *E. Young H.A. Clarke*
> *and A. Banks*
> *of this parish who died*
> *for our country 1914-1918*

Fawkham War Memorial.

William Vicris Dickinson was born in Glanhonddu, Brecon on 28 April 1856 and was educated at Cheltenham College and at the Royal Military College, Sandhurst. He started his military service as a second lieutenant in 1877 and was promoted to lieutenant and then captain in the same year of 1882. He became a major in 1892 and was then promoted to the rank of lieutenant colonel in 1902, before retiring in March 1906, having served for twenty-nine years.

At the outbreak of war in August 1914 he was appointed Assistant Adjutant General at the

General Headquarters in Rouen, France, where he died on 28 October 1917 at the age of 61 after contracting an unspecified illness whilst on active service.

He was obviously well liked and very respected by his colleagues who worked with him. His senior officer, General Graham, wrote in a letter to Dickinson's widow, Mary:

'Your husband had worked so devotedly and loyally for me ever since this war began, and I was hoping that in the New Year's Honours Gazette he would have seen how much I appreciated his services.'

Colonel Gough wrote:

'He stood alone and above everybody else in the affection of all who came in to contact with him. In the hustle and hurry of official business, friction and bickering's must have their place, but with him it was impossible. There was no one who ever had a fault to find with him and his methods; he was straight and sympathetic, and a real friend to all.'

Another officer wrote:

'The Colonel was to me like my own father (Whose guidance I never enjoyed, being only seven years old at his death), and his loving and smiling personality endeared him to me, and, in fact, to everyone of us here. I shall miss my much revered 'friend' in a way that is impossible for me to express. There is the one comfort, if it can be called such, that he fell in his battle harness, serving his dearly loved native land, the personification of one of whose greatest gentlemen he was the embodiment.'

He was created a Companion of the Order of St Michael and St George, which is an award given to individuals who have given an important service to the Empire or a foreign nation. He was also mentioned three times in despatches, by Field Marshal, Sir John French, *London Gazette*, 22 June 1915 and 1 January 1916, and by Field Marshal, Sir Douglas Haig, for gallant and distinguished service in the field, 11 December 1917.

He was married to Mary Joyce Dickinson, on 23 April 1885 and they lived at Hillside House, Fawkham in Kent. They had two sons, Douglas

Povah Dickinson, who was born 6 November 1886, and William Vicris Digby Dickinson, who was born 2 November 1889.

His late father, John Douglas Dickinson, was a retired colonel in the British Army. His widow, Mary Dickinson lived at 20 Iverna Gardens, Kensington, London.

William Vicris Dickinson is buried at the St Sever Cemetery in Rouen, France. Commonwealth army camps and hospitals were established on the outskirts of Rouen during the First World War. The 3rd Echelon General Headquarters was also stationed in the city along with a base supply depot. The city was almost overrun with hospitals. It boasted eight general hospitals, five stationary ones along with a British Red Cross hospital, a labour hospital and No.2 military Convalescent Depot,

Henry Roscoe Beddoes was a lieutenant colonel in the 4th Battalion, Royal Dublin Fusiliers, who at the time of his death on 15 January 1919, he was attached to the Regiment's 9th Battalion. His name is commemorated on the Hollybrook War Memorial in Southampton. He died whilst en route to Constantinople on board the SS *Chonia* when she sank. His body was never recovered.

According to the 1911 Census, Charles and Emma Haygreen lived at Little Wickham Cottage, Fawkham, near Lonfield, Kent, with their four children, Charley, who was the eldest, Emily, Walter and Ernest.

All three of their sons served during the war, but only Walter would survive. He was born in nearby Hartley in 1894 and before the war his occupation had been that of a gardener. Walter John Haygreen enlisted in the army on 23 November 1914 at Deptford, just before his twenty-first birthday and became a gunner (54144) in the No.4 Depot Royal Garrison Artillery. He died in Dartford in March 1938 aged just 44.

Corporal Charley Haygreen (54143), 22nd Heavy Battery, Royal Garrison Artillery enlisted at the same time as his younger brother Walter, which would also explain their consecutive service numbers. Initially he was posted to the Royal Garrison Artillery No.4 Depot in Great Yarmouth. His army service record recorded the fact that he 'Wears artificial Dentures', which was not a sufficient defect to prevent his enlistment.

The 22nd Heavy Battery arrived in France on 31 August 1915 as part of the 23rd Heavy Artillery Brigade. The original purpose of the Royal Garrison Artillery was the manning of guns of the British Empire's forts and fortresses, including coastal artillery batteries, the heavy gun batteries attached to infantry divisions, and the guns of the siege artillery.

After he was wounded, Charley was taken to the 11th Casualty Clearing Station to be treated for a shrapnel wound to his abdomen. He never recovered. By the time of his death the family home had moved to 7 Park Road, Dartford. He died of his wounds on 10 October 1917 aged 28 and is buried at the Godewaersvelde British Cemetery in the Nord region of France.

Godewaersvelde British Cemetery. (Commonwealth War Graves Commission)

The first burials at the cemetery were made by the 37th and 41st Casualty Clearing Stations in July 1917, which remained in the area until November 1917. There are 972 Commonwealth servicemen as well as 19 Germans there.

After his death, a list of his personal belongings was recorded: letters, photos, case, 2 pipes, match box cover, tobacco, tobacco pouch, silver watch (No. 234789) & chain, khaki handerkerchiefs (3), metal mirror in case, penknife, card.

Looking through army service records is always interesting as every now again they reveal information that might otherwise never have come to light. Part of a soldier's army service papers is Army Form W.5080 which includes the names and addresses of all of the deceased soldier's living relatives. In Charley's case it shows that instead of having two brothers, he in fact had five brothers and instead of only one sister, he had four.

His three other brothers were Arthur William Haygreen aged 42, James Charles aged 40 and George Charles aged 36. His three other sisters were, Jane (44), Florence (34) and Edith (32), all of whom were married. The form also showed that his brother, Ernest Harry Haygreen, is shown as being wounded and missing. The form is signed by Charley's mother Emma, and is dated 10 May 1919.

Private Ernest Harry Haygreen (R/28896), King's Royal Rifle Corps, was attached to the 2nd/16th Battalion, London Regiment (Queen's Westminster Rifles). He had previously served with the London Regiment's 18th Battalion, which was a Territorial Reserve unit, and had the service number of TR13/9112. He was just 20 years old at the time of his death. He has no known grave and his name is commemorated on the Tyne Cot War Memorial at Zonnebeke in Belgium.

It is interested to note that on the records kept on Ancestry.co.uk he is shown as having 'died of his wounds' but as his name is recorded on the Tyne Cot War Memorial this indicates that he has no known grave, so it would be difficult to know if he was killed outright or died his wounds.

Although there were numerous people with the initials of E. Young, who served in different regiments during the First World War, I was unable to come up with a definitive identity of the individual who had lived in Longfield, Kent.

Unfortunately we were unable to identify H.A. Clarke with any degree of clarity. The best we could do is to break it down to one in thirteen possible men who are shown on the CWGC website and one in six who are shown on the British Army First World War Medal Rolls index cards.

Private Albert John Banks (254528), 3rd (City of London) Battalion, London Regiment (Royal Fusiliers), lived in Longfield and enlisted at Woolwich. He was killed in action, at just 18 years of age on 8 August 1918. He is buried at the Beacon Cemetery, Sailly-Laurette, on the Somme.

The date of 8 August 1918 was significant in that it was the first day of the Battle of Amiens. The cemetery at Saint-Laurette has 772 Commonwealth graves, 258 of which are unidentified.

The 1911 Census shows Walter and Charlotte Banks living at Forge Cottage, Better Point, West Yoke, Ash, Kent, with their three children, sons Walter (14), Albert (11), and their daughter Lily (13).

It would appear however that Charlotte was a step-mother as the census showed that she and Walter had only been married for six years. A check back to the 1901 Census showed Walter's wife was then Sarah Banks, whom he had married in 1895 at Dartford.

I was unable to find any corresponding military record for Albert's brother Walter, but that is not to say that he did not serve in the military during the war. On the British Army's First World War Medal Rolls index cards system, there are more than thirty Walter and Walter T. Banks, but unfortunately it was not possible to narrow it down any more than that.

Hartley War Memorial

There are fourteen names commemorated on the Hartley War Memorial of those young men from the parish who lost their lives in the First World War. Two of them, the Haygreen brothers, Charles and Ernest, are also included on the nearby Fawkham War Memorial, which was not unusual. Quite often a man would be included on more than one of the war memorials in the district of where he was born or where he lived.

Edwin Cheary	Richard Woodward
Sidney Day	William Moore Boucher
Ernest Holness	Charles Haygreen
William Hurst	Ernest Harry Haygreen
John Rich	William James Hollands
Alec Hugh Rose	Leonard James Pinder
James Harwood Vaughan	Henry George Saunders

Gunner Edwin Cheary enlisted aged 20 years on 20 November 1914 at Maidstone, when he became a gunner (52818) in the Royal Garrison Artillery. After transferring to 'C' Company, 2nd Battalion, York and Lancaster Regiment, on 7 June 1915, he became a corporal (20502). He was awarded the Military Medal for his gallantry on 22 January 1917, but his sister, Agnes, wrote a letter to the War Office dated 16 July 1917, in which she mentioned that the actions for which he was awarded the Military Medal, took place between 20 and 22 April 1916, whilst serving in France, where he had first arrived on 18 August 1915.

When he was killed in action on 18 March 1917 he was 24 years old. On 9 July 1917, nearly four months after his death, his personal belongings were returned to his family and included a disc, letters, photos, cards, a religious book and a 25 cent note. His next-of-kin is shown as his sister, Agnes Cleary.

He is buried in the Maroc British Cemetery in Grenay, in the Pas de Calais region of France, which contains 1,379 Commonwealth graves from the First World War, 264 of which are unidentified.

His address on his attestation papers is shown as Darenth Cottages, Hartley, Longfield, Kent. The 1911 Census showed him working as a farm labourer living at Hartley with his widowed father, William Cheary, aged 63, also a farm labourer, his elder sister, Agnes (28), and his two younger brothers, Leonard and Archie.

Archie enlisted late in the war after he had turned 18 in early 1918. He was a private (32885) in the Norfolk Regiment, but unfortunately his army service record has not survived, so we do not know anything else about his time spent in the military. He died in Strood, Kent in 1940 at the relatively young age of 41.

There was no information to indicate that Leonard had served in the military. He died in 1961 in Dartford aged 66.

Private Sydney Day was born in Hartley in 1891 and when the war broke out he enlisted in the army at nearby Gravesend. He was a private (S/8074) in the 1st Battalion, Queen's Own (Royal West Kent Regiment). He first arrived in France on 26 October 1914 and was killed in action only seven months later, on 25 May 1915 during fighting on the Western Front.

Besides being awarded the British War and Victory Medals, he was also entitled to the 1914 Star. He is buried at the Perth Cemetery, China Wall, Ypres.

Perth Cemetery, China Wall, Ieper. (Commonwealth War Graves Commission)

The 1911 Census showed him living at 2 Black Lion Cottages, Hartley, Longfield, with his mother, Rebecca, and his elder brother,

Frank. A look back at the 1891 Census shows even more family. His father Charles was already 52 years of age by then and there were three other children: John (13), Kate (11), and Horace (7). The 1881 Census shows in addition, George, Albert, Frederick, Eliza and Elizabeth. I could find no record of any of Sydney's brothers having served during the war.

Corporal Ernest Holness (S/7538), 7th Battalion, Seaforth Highlanders was killed in action on the first day of the Battle of Loos on 25 September 1915. He has no known grave and his name is commemorated on the Loos War Memorial in the Pas de Calais.

The battle was the largest British offensive mounted during 1915 on the Western Front. The battle also saw the first use of poison gas by Allied forces during the war. The first day of the battle also bore witness to a remarkable act of bravery that a warrants mention even though it has no connection to Ernest Holness.

Daniel Logan Laidlaw had previously served in the British Army for sixteen years between 1896 and 1912 during which time he had served with the Durham Light Infantry in India before transferring to the King's Own Scottish Borderers, the regiment in which his elder brother served. At the age of 40 he re-enlisted in 1915, once again serving in the King's Own Scottish Borderers, as a piper in the 7th Battalion.

On the very first day of the battle on 25 September 1915, at a position that was known as Hill 70, prior to an assault on enemy trenches and during the worst of the bombardment, Piper Laidlaw, seeing that his company was shaken with the effects of gas, and with complete disregard for his own safety, climbed up on to the parapet of the trench and began marching up and down playing his pipes. The effect of his act of unbelievable bravery was immediate, causing the rest of his company to climb out of the trench and attack the German positions ahead of them. He continued playing his pipes even after he was wounded and the German position had been taken. For his heroic action that day he was awarded the Victoria Cross.

Rifleman William John Hurst (R/24244), 9th Battalion, King's Royal Rifle Corps was killed in action on 15 September 1916, aged 32.

He is buried it the Guards Cemetery, Lesboeufs on the Somme.

There are 3,136 servicemen buried in the cemetery. A staggering 1,643 of these have no identity.

Guards Cemetery, Lesboeufs. (Commonwealth War Graves Commission)

After the war his parents, Joseph and Elizabeth Hurst, lived at Hartley Green, Longfield, Kent, although in the 1911 Census William was a boarder living at 10 E.C. Powder Cottages, E.C. Powder Works, Bean, near Dartford, with a Mr and Mrs Flemming.

Lance Corporal John Rich was born in Hartley, enlisted in the army at nearby Gravesend and eventually became a lance corporal (23490) in the 1st Battalion, Gloucestershire Regiment, which at the outbreak of the war was based at Bordon in Hampshire as part of the 3rd Brigade, 1st Division.

He arrived at Le Havre with his battalion on 13 August 1914 and was killed in action on 9 September 1916. The day before John died his battalion, which was stationed at The Quadrangle to the south-west of Mametz Wood, was preparing for an attack on an area known as High Wood. The men of the 1st Battalion began the short journey to the assembly trenches to the south of High Wood at 12 noon, but quickly began to sustain casualties when British artillery accidentally began shelling the Gloucesters' positions because their shells were dropping too short. After the mistake was reported the shelling stopped only to be re-started half an hour later with the same devastating results, as once again the shells were dropping short of their intended target. The problem was eventually sorted out by which time the Gloucesters had incurred numerous casualties both wounded and dead.

When the attack began in earnest the advancing British troops were met by stiff German resistance from both rifle and machine-gun fire and, despite some success, the assault was called off at 1945 hours, mainly because of a lack of available reinforcements.

The next day saw the Battle of Ginchy which was one of the numerous battles which made up the Battle of the Somme.

1st Gloucestershire Regiment at Bordon Hampshire, 1914.

John's name is commemorated on the Thiepval Memorial on the Somme.

The 1911 Census shows John living with his parents, John and Ellen Rich, along with his brother, Joseph, at 3 Black Lion Cottages, Hartley, Near Longfield, Kent. He was the next door neighbour of Sydney Day, who is also mentioned in this chapter, who lived at 2 Black Lion Cottages.

There was no absolute direct match for Joseph Rich having served in the First World War, but searching through the British Army's First World War Medal Rolls index cards, there were in fact seven with the name Joseph Rich who served with different regiments during the First World War, so it is more than probable that the Joseph who we are looking for, is one of them.

Private Alec Hugh Rose was born in Offchurch, Warwickshire, lived in Hartley, Kent and enlisted in the army in London. He was a private (M2/020930) in the 74th Divisional Mechanical Transport Company, Army Service Corps, when he was killed in action on 14 September 1918.

He is buried at the St Sever Cemetery Extension, Rouen, in the Seine-Maritime region of France.

According to the 1911 Census he lived with his parents Thomas and Fanny Rose, along with his two younger sisters, Minnie and Gladys, and his Aunt Maria, at Fairby Cottages, Hartley, Longfield, Dartford. The census also showed that Thomas and Fanny had five other children, the assumption therefore being that they were all older than Alec, Minnie and Gladys.

Rifleman James Harwood Vaughan was born in Eynesbury, Huntingdonshire in 1880. During the war he enlisted in the army as a rifleman (6084) in 1st/16th (County of London) Battalion, London Regiment (Queen's Westminster Rifles. Aged 36, he was killed in action on 1 October 1916, which was the first day of the Battle of the Transloy Ridges. His name is commemorated on the Thiepval Memorial, on the Somme.

The 1911 Census shows James living at 201 Kings Hall Road, Beckenham, Kent, along with an uncle, two sisters and a young servant. He was single and worked as a clerk. After the war his parents, Frederic and Clara Vaughan, lived at Hartley Hall Cottage, Hartley, Longfield, Dartford.

Private Richard Woodward (18159), Reserve Battalion, Grenadier Guards died on 13 November 1918 and had been medically discharged from the army prior to his death for no longer being physically fit enough for war service. He is buried in All Saints Churchyard in Hartley.

His parents, James and Jessica Woodward, lived at 4 Black Lion Cottages, Hartley, Longfield, Kent. This meant that three families who lived next door to each other in Hartley, at numbers two, three and four, named Day, Rich and Woodward, had all lost sons to the war.

Captain William Moore Boucher was the son of Elizabeth Boucher who lived at Sacristy Cottage, Hartley, Longfield, Kent. His late father was from South Africa. During the First World War William was a captain in the 6th Battalion, Queen's Own (Royal West Kent Regiment), when he was killed in action on 20 November 1917 aged 21.

He is buried at the Fifteen Ravine British Cemetery, in the Nord region of France. William's name is also commemorated on the Cobham War Memorial.

Serjeant William James Hollands was an acting serjeant (53453) in 'D' Battery, 80 Brigade, Royal Horse Artillery and Royal Field Artillery. The battery arrived in France on 14 July 1915 and William was killed in action on 17 February 1916, aged 32. He is buried at the Lijssenthoek Military Cemetery in Poperinghe in Belgium. His name is also commemorated on the Wrotham War Memorial.

In the 1911 Census, William is shown as being a lodger with Joseph and Rose Ebbs and their son William, at Mym Wood Lodge, Bell Bar, Hatfield in Hertfordshire. His occupation is shown as a gamekeeper. His parents, Alfred and Eliza Hollands, lived at the Railway Tavern, Longfield, Kent.

William is a good example of how it was determined whose name would be commemorated on war memorials. He was born in Hartley and grew up there, but by the time of the 1911 Census he was living in Hatfield and his parents lived in Longfield, Dartford after the war. His name is commemorated on the Hartley war memorial as well as the one at Wrotham, the inference being that at some time he must have lived there. There was no hard and fast set of rules about how it was decided whose name would appear on a particular memorial. It was simply left for those who had come up with the idea and the funding for the memorial to decide what criteria they would use.

There was a sad twist to this particular story as the Ebb's son William, also joined the army soon after the start of the war. He became a private (G/2737) in the 4th Battalion, London Regiment (Royal Fusiliers) and was killed in action on 27 March 1916 aged 24, whilst serving on the Western Front. This was the first day of the action at St Eloi craters, which would continue until 16 April 1916. The British had tunnelled under the German trenches and at the same time that the mines were detonated at 0415 hours on 27 March, there was also the beginning of an artillery bombardment. William's battalion were up and out of their trenches less than a minute later, but unlike the 1st Battalion, Northumberland Fusiliers who made it to the German lines with the loss of only one man, the 4th Royal Fusiliers came under immediate and intense German machine-gun fire as soon as they left their trenches. Sadly, William was one of those that died.

Airman 2nd Class Leonard James Pinder, Royal Flying Corps died on 22 February 1917 aged 30. He is buried in the Aldershot Military Cemetery, Hampshire, which would suggest that he had been treated at the military hospital in Aldershot prior to his death.

After the war his mother, who by now had re-married, was living at 'Hillcrest', Hartley, Kent, whilst his widow, was living at 15 Trossachs Road, East Dulwich, London.

Petty Officer Henry George Saunders was born in Peckham, London on 18 November 1881. He enlisted after the outbreak of the war and became a petty officer (194067) in the Royal Navy and was attached to HM Submarine *E32*, when he died on 1 April 1917 as a result of a drowning accident, aged 35. He has no known grave and his name is commemorated on the Portsmouth Naval Memorial.

E Class submarines had a crew of thirty. We know that the E32 was launched on 16 August 1916 and was commissioned in October 1916. She survived the war and was finally sold off on 6 September 1922.

His father, Henry John Saunders, was living at Church Road, Hartley, Longfield, Kent, after the war.

Sutton-at-Hone – War Memorial

There are the names of forty-nine brave souls, who lost their lives in the fighting of the First World War, commemorated on the war memorial in the grounds of St John the Baptist Church at Sutton-at-Hone.

Sutton-at-Hone War Memorial.

F. Archer

A. Bourne

F.E. Bowers

G.H. Barton

F. Brown

W.T. Birch

L. Busbridge

W. Chambers

E.T. Crees

A. Crowhurst

A.G. Course

A. Edney

Charles Elliot

William Elliot

H.W. Friend

W.J. Gibbs

W. Green

A.A. Garrett

P.J. Henry

W.J. Wood

W. Harvey

A.O. Mayne

G.W. Mayne

A. Mankey

H. Mullender

W.G. Nettleingham

T.H. Ovenden

W. Parish

A.C. Pocknall

A.A. Robinson

H.K. Smith

G. Tompkins

J. Tingle

W. Williams

C.A. Rayner

C.A. Reynolds

F.N. Reynolds

L. Willet

C. Woodgate

A.G. Wright

A.G. Warner

J.H. West

J.E. Whalin

E.G Wharton

C.W. Turner

H.G. Vesse

W.A. Waterman

W.R. Waterman

A.H. West

Rifleman W.G. Nettleingham is buried at the Sutton-at-Hone burial ground which adjoins the St John the Baptist's Churchyard. He was a rifleman (60091) in the King's Royal Rifle Corps when he died aged 25 on 23 February 1919. Because of the date of his death, he either died from his wounds or an illness such as the flu pandemic.

He was a married man and lived at 3 Coles Cottages, Shire Hall Road, Hawley, Dartford. Unfortunately no military records have survived for a person with this name and initials who served with the King's Royal Rifle Corps.

A search of the 1911 Census for the surname of Nettleingham came up with a William Nettleingham who was born in Gravesend in 1899 which would have made him only 20 at the time of his death rather than 25.

Private Albert Charles Pocknall attested for military service on 9 December 1915. He then spent the next fifteen months on the Army Reserve before being called up on 26 March 1917. Initially he became a private and was posted to the 43rd Training Reserve Battalion before being transferred to the 'B' Company, 2nd Battalion, Norfolk Regiment as a private (31067) on 16 June 1917. He arrived in Basra on 18 August 1917 with his new battalion who were based at a camp in Mirjana. On 11 August 1917 he was admitted to hospital for two days, suffering with exhaustion. He died on 10 June 1918.

His army service record shows initially he was reported as, 'missing believed drowned in the Dialah river'. As his body was never recovered, the date of his death 'was assumed for official purposes'.

On 8 May 1918, Lieutenant Colonel F. Higson, who was the commanding officer of the 2nd Battalion, Norfolk Regiment had issued a Battalion Order for guidance and strict compliance regarding the issue of soldiers bathing in the sea. It covered the times and locations where bathing was permitted. Even though there were specific company 'bathing parades', as they were called, individual bathing was still encouraged, 'although it is advisable that men do not bathe in parties of less than three, and that these men should have passed a test proving they are capable of remaining afloat in deep water for a minimum of five minutes. All ranks should be encouraged to pass this test'.

The order also included the need for improvised rafts to be built and kept in the bathing areas in case of accidents. It would appear that Albert's death was down to nothingmore sinister than a tragic swimming accident. His death was taken so seriously that an official court of enquiry was held on 26 July 1918 in Basra before Captain S. Hallam, and second lieutenants A.M. Richardson and G.A. Mitchell. All three officers were members of the 2nd Battalion, Norfolk Regiment.

Four witnesses gave evidence before the hearing: the Acting Company Sergeant Major 14247 W.N. Marshall, Private 31073 B. Woodard, Private 23642 W.B. Riches and Corporal 19126 H. Cushion.

Privates Woodard and Riches gave evidence that, along with Private

Pocknall, all three of them had gone to the river to wash their clothes, and that whilst there Pocknall stated he was going to take a bathe. Woodard and Riches carried on with their washing and only when they had finished did they notice that Pocknall was missing.

Company Sergeant Major Marshall confirmed that Woodard and Riches had informed him at about 6.40pm that Pocknall was missing and that after informing his company commander, (who was neither named in the report nor called to give evidence at the enquiry), he was instructed to commence a search for Pocknall, which he duly did at 7pm and again at 3.30am the following morning.

Corporal Cushion gave evidence that on 8 May 1918 he read out the Battalion Order regarding bathing, to his company (B) and that a copy of it was also posted on the company notice board later that day. Lieutenant Colonel F. Higson was not called to give evidence confirming he was the person who had issued the Battalion Order, or why he had seen the need to issue it in the first place.

After hearing all of the evidence from the four witnesses the Court of Enquiry came up with the following statement:

'After hearing the evidence of the witnesses in this case, the Court is of the opinion that No. 31067 Private Pocknall, 2nd Battalion, Norfolk Regiment met his death by drowning in the Dialah river through neglecting to obey Battalion Order Annexure 8 of the 8-5-18, a copy of which is attached to the proceedings of this Court.'

As his body was never discovered and he has no known grave, his name is commemorated on the Basra War Memorial in Iraq which has more than 40,000 names of Commonwealth servicemen commemorated on it. In the main these names relate to those British, Commonwealth and other Allied soldiers who died in operations in Mesopotamia (Iraq) from September 1914 through until the end of August 1921.

The memorial was unveiled on 27 March 1929 by Brigadier General Sir Gilbert Falkingham Clayton KCMG KBE CB. During the First World War he worked as an intelligence officer in Cairo, serving in the newly formed Arab Bureau. He supervised those who worked to start the Arab revolt, turning the Arabs against their Ottoman rulers, and T.E. Lawrence (Laurence of Arabia) mentions him in his 1935 book, *Seven Pillars of Wisdom.*

Private Herbert George Vesse was born in Elmstead in Essex in 1883. The 1911 Census showed that he lived at 'Homefield', Sutton-at-Hone, Kent, with the Potts family, where he was employed as a gardener and his sister Annie was employed as a servant.

Herbert enlisted in the army at Woolwich, becoming a private (201612) in the 4th Battalion, Essex Regiment, which was a Territorial Unit. He was posted to the Egyptian theatre of war, where he was killed in action on 26 March 1917 in Palestine. He is buried in the Gaza War Cemetery.

Herbert was a married man and after the war his widow, Lilian Mary Vesse, was living at 9 Barfield Terrace, Sutton-at-Hone, Dartford. In his will he left her £170 18 shillings.

Herbert's brother, Percy, who was thirteen years younger than him, also served in the military during the First World War. He initially enlisted as a private (16797) in the Essex Regiment, but later transferred to The King's (Liverpool) Regiment, also as a private (325040), first arriving in France on 9 June 1915 when he was still only 19 years of age. He survived the war, and died in 1985, aged 90.

Rifleman Albert Edney (C/9707), 20th Battalion, King's Royal Rifle Corps was 27 years old when he was killed in action on 4 May 1917. His mother, Mrs Mary Edney, lived at Homefield Farm, Sutton-at-Hone, Dartford.

Albert is buried at the Tilloy British Cemetery at Tilloy-lès-Mofflaines, which is situated in the Pas de Calais. The cemetery was begun in April 1917 and initially contained graves from the following months. Later burials were added throughout 1918, although the nearby

Tilloy British Cemetery.

village of Tilloy-lès-Mofflaines was taken and held by the Germans between March and August 1918. After the Armistice further burials followed when those initially buried at nearby smaller locations, were moved to the Tilloy Cemetery which now contains 1,642 graves of Commonwealth servicemen. Of these 611 remain unidentified.

Private Clements Arthur Reynolds (G/4141), 6th Battalion, Queen's Own (Royal West Kent Regiment) was killed on 9 March 1916, aged 23. He has no known grave and his name is commemorated on the War Memorial at Loos in the Pas de Calais.

The 1911 Census shows that Clements lived at The Street, Lower Sutton-at-Hone, Dartford with his mother Catherine and his younger sister Mabel.

His army service record has survived allowing us to find out about his time in the military. He enlisted very early on in the war, on 19 October 1914, joining at Gravesend. Amongst the papers in his service record was a letter which had been written on behalf of his mother and sent to the Army Records office at Hounslow in late March 1916:

> '*I am writing on behalf of the widowed mother of the above soldier whose death occurred on the 9th March 1916. She has heard from his officer some time ago of his death but so far no official notice has been sent to her. Can you confirm the death of the above named soldier?*'

Besides the obvious sadness attached to that letter it also showed in part what families and friends went through in an emotional sense during the war. Here was a mother who knew that her son had been killed as she had received word from his commanding officer informing her as such; but perhaps because of nothing more than a clerical oversight on behalf of the War Office, she had heard nothing official. It was as if she needed to receive the official notification of her son's death before she could fully accept her loss.

One of the other documents showed that Clements had two older brothers, Charles and Albert as well as five sisters, Mabel, Florence, Harriet, Anne and Alvey. His mother was sent her son's award of the 1914-15 Star, which she received on 9 August 1919. It would be nearly another two years before she received his British War and Victory Medals on 14 July 1921.

Company Sergeant Major Francis Neave Reynolds was a 37-year-old married man with four children living at 19 Queen Street, Wombwell, Yorkshire, when he enlisted in the army on 23 September 1914 as a private (13/917) in the 13th Battalion, York and Lancaster Regiment. The same day he was promoted to the rank of sergeant and seven months later on 2 April 1915 he was once again promoted, this time to company sergeant major, an extremely quick climb up the ladder of promotion. It is quite possible that he had previous military experience prior to enlisting.

He was killed in action on 17 July 1916 and is buried at the Rue-du-Bacquerot No.1 Military Cemetery, Laventie in the Pas de Calais.

Rue-du-Bacquerot No.1 Military Cemetery, Laventie.

Unfortunately some of the writing on his army service record is very faint, but it would appear that he had three brothers and five sisters all from the Dartford area. After the war, Francis's widow Martha, moved to Lower Sutton, Sutton-at-Hone, Dartford, possibly to be closer to other family members who lived nearby, including Francis's mother Catherine Jane Reynolds, who lived at Sutton-at-Hone. Martha was awarded an army widow's pension of 27/- a week for herself and her four children, which began on 5 February 1917.

Private Edward Thomas Crees was born in Folkestone in 1892 to Thomas and Ann Crees, although his mother unfortunately passed away in January 1910, leaving Thomas to bring up five children, three of them under nine years of age.

The 1911 Census showed the family living at 13 Queensberry Mews East, South Kensington, London SW. Thomas's occupation was shown as a foreman, although of what it does not say, but whatever it was paid him well enough for him to be able to employ a servant, Myra or Mary Elsom. Checking the actual census document shows that originally she was recorded as being a visitor and 14-year-old Edith Elsom was shown as her daughter. This was later changed so that Mary was then shown as a servant and Edith as being a visitor. Thomas had three sons, Edward (16), Percy (13) and Gordon (8). His two daughters were Daisy (6) and Hilda (2).

Both Edward and Percy served in the war. Edward was 22 years of age when he enlisted in London on 8 September 1914 and became a private (MS/4070) in the 50th Auxiliary Bus Corps, Army Service Corps. Initially he signed a 'Short Service Attestation', which meant he had only agreed to join the army for one year, but even so, he stayed on regardless. Before the war his occupation had been that of a lorry driver, which was not too far removed from what he found himself called upon to do once in the army.

He arrived in France on 7 October 1914, less than a month after he had enlisted and, except for a couple of furloughs for leave, he remained on active service in France until the day of his death. One of the pages of his army service record clearly states that he died on 5 November 1917 at the 26th General Hospital, Étaples from a 'GSW' (gunshot wound) to his right leg. Although there is no detailed information about what actually happened, what is clear from reading through it, is that he was not shot in fighting with the Germans. His injuries are recorded as being of an 'accidental nature'. This was somewhat confusing trying to establish, without just guessing, how he might have been accidentally shot in the leg, and by whom.

A court of enquiry was held in to his death at Étaples on 20 November 1917, with the finding of the court being; 'Accidental injuries whilst on duty', but once again, there was no detailed explanation of how it was he came to be shot. It is only on looking through the pages of the Court of Enquiry that there is a detailed explanation of what actually happened, but instead of clarifying matters, all it does is confuse things even more. The following is the content of a statement that was made by Private M2/149450, 50th Auxiliary Omnibus Company, which is actually the same unit as Edward. The statement is dated 18 October 1917.

> *SIR,*
>
> *Below you will find my statement giving particulars as to how the accident occurred between MS/4070 Pte. Crees, ET Motor cyclist, and lorry No. 23410 which I was driving at the time. Both concerned belonged to No. 50 Aux. Omnibus Company.*
>
> *This is how the accident happened: I was out on duty with convoy (troop carrying), having 17 passengers aboard when the accident took place at a point between SYLVESTRE-CAPPEL and STEENVOORDE, on Wednesday October 17th, 1917, at about 7.15 am.*
>
> *I was travelling in the direction of STEENVOORDE, speed about 10 miles per hour, when motor cyclist travelling in same direction attempted to pass me on left hand side; he got about three yards ahead of my lorry when he made for the centre of the road and in doing so his cycle skidded and he fell in front of my lorry near the right hand front wheel; I at once applied my brakes and turned my lorry near the left hand side of the road trying to avoid running over the cyclist, but my chance was hopeless.*
>
> *Pte. A Minch*
> *M2/149450 MT – ASC*
> *No. 50 Aux. Omnibus Company.'*

There was another statement attached to the file from a Private

M2/148753 Scadwell, who was the front seat passenger in the lorry and who corroborated what Private Minch had said in his statement.

It is somewhat confusing how Edward's army service record clearly states that he accidentally sustained a gunshot wound to his right leg, whilst the paperwork attached to the court of enquiry clearly states that he was accidentally run over by a lorry driven by one of his own colleagues.

Private Percy Crees was born in 1897 at 2 Queensberry Mews East, South Kensington, London, SW. He enlisted at Hammersmith on 11 May 1915 and was three years younger than his brother Edward. He began his military service as a 17-year-old private (4370) in the 7th (City of London) Battalion, London Regiment. After he had completed his initial training he left from Southampton on 9 March 1916 and arrived in Le Havre the next day.

Whilst in France on 5 August 1916 he was admitted to hospital, although his army service record is not clear about why or where he attended hospital. It could have been No. 2 Stationary Hospital. Four days later on 9 August 1916 he was moved to the 13th General Hospital which appears to have been at Abbeville. On 12 August 1916 his condition was deemed to be so serious that he had to be sent home to England on board the Hospital Ship *Panama*. On his arrival he was sent to the military hospital in Bermondsey in London. The doctors could find no heart murmurs but noticed that he had a nasal obtrusion on the right side of his face which was to do with his adenoids, a condition for which he had already been operated on three times before he had joined the army. Doctors believed that his condition had been brought on by strain. He was reclassified as not being suitable to fight but not discharged, instead being transferred to a non-combat type role.

During the five months he spent in France he had to fall out of marches on several occasions due to shortness of breath and pain over his heart. On 1 July 1917 he transferred to the Sussex Regiment. On 26 July he transferred to the Middlesex Regiment. On 18 May 1917 he transferred to the 5th Battalion, Labour Corps, before transferring to the 387th Battalion of the same regiment, as private 153956. He was finally demobilized from the army on 15 May 1919 in Nottingham. He died in 1950 in Bromley, Kent. In the years immediately after the end of the war, his widow lived at 3 Catherine Place, Sutton-at-Hone, Kent.

Private George William Mayne (6546), 1st/5th Battalion, Northumberland Fusiliers, was killed in action on 15 November 1916. He has no known grave and his name is commemorated on the Thiepval Memorial on the Somme.

His parents, William Henry and Martha Mayne, lived at 19 St Johns Terrace, Sutton-at-Hone, Dartford. In the years after the war, George's widow, Alice, who was now using the surname Hawes, was living at Laburnham Cottage, Norton, Bury St Edmunds. Many women, whose husbands were killed during the First World War, re-married. Some because they had found a new love and others because they had children, nowhere to live, or would have found it difficult to survive without a man to support them. This was a time when the welfare state in was in its infancy and workhouses were still in existence, as they were up until the mid-1930s.

Rifleman Arthur Owen Mayne (C/7616), 18th Battalion, King's Royal Rifle Corps was born in Dartford and enlisted at Kingsway in Middlesex at which time he was living at Swanley in Kent. He was killed on 3 October 1916 at the Battle of the Transloy Ridges, which took place between 1 and 20 October 1916. He was 28 years of age.

The 18th Battalion, which was raised at Gidea Park in Romford, on 4 June 1915, was also known as the Arts and Crafts Battalion, raised by Major Sir Herbert Raphael. He was a man of many talents: a noted promoter of the Arts and Crafts movement, MP for South Derbyshire as well as local magistrate. He had made his money from banking.

The regiment was one of the British Army's élite units and men flocked to join it from all over the country; but it also had a particular appeal to young men from the Midlands where Sir Hebert had his main support.

Arthur has no known grave and his name is commemorated on the Thiepval Memorial on the Somme. His parents Henry and Mary Ann Mayne, lived in Clement Street, Swanley, Kent.

Private Arthur Mankey was born in Shoreham, Kent in 1893. Before the war he was a builder's labourer which meant he was already extremely fit. He enlisted in the army on 4 November 1914 and became a private (G/2066) in the 7th Battalion, Queen's Own (Royal West Kent Regiment).

His attestation papers show that he had originally only signed up for what was known as a 'Short Service' term of 'three years with the Colours', enlisting at Woolwich. His army service record shows that after having completed his initial training in England, he arrived in France on 26 July 1915. Less than a year later he would officially be reported as missing presumed dead. He was reported as being missing on 13 July 1916, which was less than two weeks in to the Battle of the Somme. Beneath that entry on the same page it goes on to say, 'Death Presumed 13.7.16. Killed in action or died of wounds on or about 13 July 1916 – Expeditionary Force France.'

It just emphasises the confusion that reigned when a soldier's body was never recovered in battle. As Arthur could have just as easily been taken prisoner it would be fair to assume that this particular entry was recorded retrospectively, and after they had already checked with the German authorities.

His parents, John and Hepzibah Mankey, lived at 1 Granville Terrace, Shire Hall Road, Hawley, Dartford, along with their six other sons and three daughters. We could find no record for five of Arthur's brothers having served during the First World War, but did manage to find an army service record for Silas. He originally enlisted at Aldershot on 17 November 1914, joining the Army Service Corps as a private (T/4036093). He lasted for only six days before being 'discharged in consequence of being not likely to become an efficient soldier'. He was obviously a determined fellow who had a strong desire to do his bit for king and country, because a year later on 3 December 1915 he re-enlisted at Dartford and was taken on as a private (TR/9/17526) to the 43rd Training Reserve Battalion located in Warminster.

On 27 March 1917, having obviously proved that he could become an efficient soldier, he transferred to the 2nd Battalion, Norfolk Regiment as a private (311107) and four months later on 15 July, he arrived at Basra in Mesopotamia. He eventually returned to England on 28 March 1919 and was demobilized on 26 April and placed on the Army Reserve, his particular war having literarily turned full circle.

Private William A. Waterman (1513) (203190), 2nd/4th Battalion, Queen's Own (Royal West Kent Regiment) was killed in action on 8

May 1917 at just 20 years of age. He is buried at the Gaza War Cemetery.

His parents, Alfred and Kate Waterman, lived at Allchins Cottage, Sutton-at-Hone, Dartford.

Private William Robert Waterman (L/11145), 1st Battalion, Queen's Own (Royal West Kent Regiment) was killed in action on 4 October 1917 during the Third Battle of Ypres, aged 20. He has no known grave and his name is commemorated on the Tyne Cot War Memorial which is situated in Zonnebeke, Belgium.

William's mother, Mrs E. Waterman, lived at Kennards Yard, Sutton-at-Hone, Dartford.

Rifleman Lewis Busbridge (2089), 'E' Company, 4th Battalion, Rifle Brigade had enlisted in the army at Woolwich, a month before his nineteenth birthday on 8 May 1907, signing on for twelve years.

He had only been in the army for one month when he needed an operation for a hernia which required him to remain in Woolwich hospital for thirty days. He had been out of hospital for less than two weeks when he once again injured his hernia which required further hospital treatment. This was not the end of his medical treatment. Between 10 May 1908 and 8 November 1909 whilst serving in Egypt, he was in hospital on five separate occasions for a total of ninety-two days, to be treated for sexually transmitted diseases, including syphilis and gonorrhoea.

He arrived in France on 20 December 1914 but was killed in action on 14 May 1915. He has no known grave and his name is commemorated on the Ypres (Menin Gate) Memorial.

On 16 March 1919 Mrs L. Moore, Lewis's sister, who at the time was living at 2 Bank Houses, Hawley, near Dartford, and who had previously lived at Kennards Cottages, Sutton-at-Hone, Dartford, applied for the 1914 Star in respect of his war time services only to be advised that he did not meet the required criteria which required him to have served in France or Belgium between 5 August and 23 November 1914. However, he was awarded the 1914-1915 Star along with the British War and Victory Medals.

Private Leonard Willet was born in Barming near Maidstone, Kent in 1897. He enlisted in the army on 22 November 1915 at Camberwell aged 18, and became a private (L/11146) in the 11th (Service) Battalion, Queen's Own (Royal West Kent Regiment), known as the Lewisham Pals.

He arrived in France on 29 December 1915, which meant his initial training had taken less than thirty-seven days. He was killed on 15 September 1916, the first day of the Battle of Flers-Courcelette during the Somme offensive. The battle marked the first ever use of tanks in war, when the British used forty-nine of them to try and gain a decisive victory against the Germans, which they did. Leonard is commemorated on the Thiepval Memorial, on the Somme.

Before the war, he lived at Homefield Farm, Sutton-at-Hone, near Dartford, with his parents, William and Dorothy Willett, along with one of their two remaining sons, and one of their two daughters.

CHAPTER THIRTEEN

German Prisoners of War

In the earlier chapter in this book on military hospitals, we see that the Lower Southern Military Hospital in Dartford catered for wounded and injured German prisoners of war. After being treated there, they were then sent to prisoner of war camps in different parts of the country depending on where there were vacancies for them. One such group of prisoners were sent from Dartford to Skipton in North Yorkshire.

In 1914 there was a military area called Raikeswood Camp, in what is now Salisbury Street, which was used by the 16th and 18th Battalions of the West Yorkshire Regiment (Prince of Wales's Own), known locally as the Bradford Pals. After they left the camp it was used as a prisoner-of-war camp from January 1918 for captured German soldiers, and housed some 500 officers and 130 soldiers from the other ranks. The camp remained in use until October 1919, when the last of the prisoners held there were finally repatriated to Germany.

On 21 April 1921 an article appeared in *The Times Literary Supplement* under the headline, 'A Yorkshire Prisoner of War Camp from within'. It was about a book which had been published in Germany by a group of Imperial German officers who had been interned at Skipton during the First World War.

The book included some of their likes and dislikes about the camp. They were more than happy with their overall treatment by their British guards and were suitably impressed with the camp's hospital and medical services. They were less happy about their accommodation huts, which they found to be very draughty; one would imagine that this applied even more so in the winter months, coupled with the fact that they didn't think they received a sufficient supply of fuel.

Their biggest complaint was saved for the belief that their British captors were actually being impertinent to detain German officers in the first place.

In February and March 1919 the camp was greatly affected by the flu pandemic which was sweeping the world at that time; so badly that 105 of them were sent to the nearby British military hospital at Keighley for treatment. Five of them died en route from Skipton to Keighley whilst a further forty-two died in hospital.

On 16 August 1918 a group of six German officers were moved from the Lower Southern Hospital in Dartford to the prisoner of war camp in Skipton. One of the officers, Hauptmann von Kühlewein, was so incensed at the way he felt that he and his colleagues had been treated on the journey that when he was repatriated back to Germany, in December 1918 he wrote a letter of complaint to the German Foreign office.

'On 16th August 1918 on the occasion of their journey from Dartford to Skipton camp, which necessitated four changes, the following wounded officers had to carry their entire baggage including some heavy pieces, and although a man with a cart and a British Sergeant accompanying the party offered their assistance, the officer in charge would not permit the proffered aid to be availed of.

Leutnant Jung – Amputated foot.
Leutnant Johrol – Open wound on neck.
Leutnant Langner – Shot in lung.
Leutnant Luecke – Injuries to face.
Leutnant Paschkewitz – Bladder trouble.
Hauptmann von Kühlewein – Amputated arm.

On one occasion we had load up our luggage on a cart and drive it ourselves. Leutnant Jung had to hang a fairly heavy cardboard box on each crutch and Leutnant Johrol, notwithstanding the wound in his neck, had to carry on his shoulder a sack of clothing standing at least 1m high. My representations to the officer in charge were of no effect.'

The German Foreign Office forwarded Hauptmann von Kühlewein's letter on to the Swiss Legation with the following request:

'The (German) Foreign Office requests the Swiss Legation to protest to the British Government against such unworthy treatment of German prisoner of war officers, demanding assurances that such occurrences shall not be repeated in the future.

The Foreign Office will feel grateful to the Swiss Legation for transmission of the reply of the British Government.

Berlin, 12th December 1918'

A month later on 14 January 1919 the Swiss Legation in London sent the following letter to the Secretary of State for Foreign Affairs, along with a copy of Hauptmann von Kühlewein's letter of complaint.

SWISS LEGATION (GERMAN DIVISION)
9 Carlton House Terraces
London SW1
IMMEDIATE
The Swiss Min(49). **Rue-du-Bacquerot No.1 Military Cemetery, Laventie.***ster presents his compliments to His Britannic Majesty's Principal Secretary of State for Foreign Affairs, and has the honour to transmit herewith a copy of a Note Verbale of the German Foreign Office. No. IIIb 36257 178780 dated December 2 1918, received through the Departement Politique Suisse at Berne, containing a statement alleged to have been made by Hauptmann von Kühlewein, who arrived in Germany on November 1st, 1918 with a transport of seriously wounded prisoners from England, concerning the treatment of certain German officer prisoners of war on the occasion of their transfer from Dartford to Skipton camp.*

The German Foreign Office protests against the treatment described in the accompanying Note Verbale and desires that a statement be obtained from His Majesty's Government to the end that a repetition of the alleged occurrences may be prevented.

Monsieur Carlin will be happy to transmit to Berlin, through the Department Politique Suisse, the substance of any reply that His Majesty's Government may desire to make.

14th January 1919.'

There is no record of what, if any, reply was sent by the British Government to the German Foreign Office in Berlin.

CHAPTER FOURTEEN

Belgian Refugees

At the start of the war the Germany Army began its march through Belgium to attack their French neighbours, and this in turn led to an exodus of Belgian nationals who had no desire to stay behind and face an uncertain future at the hands of their German invaders.

With the war only a matter of weeks old, in September 1914, a quarter of a million Belgians invaded the shores of the south coast of England to escape an ever-advancing German Army. The first Belgian refugees to arrive in Dartford did so in October 1914 and were initially accommodated in the less than salubrious surroundings of the workhouse at West Hill.

There had been military posturing going on throughout Europe during most of the nineteenth century which came to a head as the dawning of a new millennium fast approached. This led to countries signing treaties with other nations in an effort to protect themselves from the threat of invasion from those they saw as more powerful and aggressive neighbours. The British Government had signed the Treaty of London in 1830 and made a commitment to Belgium, a commitment which had ultimately led to a war with Germany.

Never before had Britain had to deal with such a large movement of foreign nationals into its midst. It was a massive undertaking, a logistical nightmare for the British Government which had to deal with the initial reception and registration of all these refugees. They had to be housed and fed, either with the assistance of local authorities or the help of affluent benefactors. After the war ended most Belgians returned to their homeland, even though it was to an uncertain future.

Most refugees were warmly accepted into the numerous communities to which they were sent. The British people felt an immediate empathy and a warmness towards them; why is not clear, but in some places it did not last. Maybe it was because the belief that the war would be over by Christmas did not materialise. It was like having relatives who had come to visit but then out-stayed their welcome, but with most of its men either at the front or in training to go to war, the British government needed able bodied young men to help in its war effort, and many Belgian refugees found work in munitions factories such those situated in and around Dartford.

The demand for munitions meant that the output at the Dartford Vickers factory more than quadrupled, which not surprisingly had a very positive effect on the local economy. Besides the munitions industry, Dartford also had a large chemical factory in the shape of Burroughs Wellcome, which made the town a centre for the pharmaceutical industry. The company would later go on to become part of the massive, GlaxoSmithKline Empire.

Besides the refugees, Britain also took in some 25,000 wounded Belgium soldiers and treated them in their hospitals and convalescent homes, on top of that there were, at one stage of the war, some 150,000 Belgian soldiers training in Britain, waiting to return and defend their country against the German aggressor.

A statue by the Belgian sculptor, Victor Rousseau, was unveiled at Victoria Embankment Gardens in the City of London on 12 October 1920 in a ceremony attended by the Belgian Prime Minister and members of the Belgian Royal family. It was a token of their gratitude and appreciation for what the British nation had done for them during the First World War.

CHAPTER FIFTEEN

The Queen's Own
(Royal West Kent Regiment)

The Queen's Own (Royal West Kent Regiment) was an amalgamation of the 50th (Queen's Own) Regiment of Foot and the 97th (Earl of Ulster's) Regiment of Foot and came into being on 1 July 1881 as a result of what was known as the Childers Reforms, which in essence created a network of multi-battalion regiments.

It was formed as an infantry regiment of the British Army and survived until 1961 when it amalgamated with the Buffs (Royal East Kent Regiment) to become the Queen's Own Buffs, The Royal Kent Regiment.

The 1st/5th Battalion, The Queen's Own (Royal West Kent) Regiment was a Territorial Unit which was formed at Bromley in August 1914 and two months later on 30 October 1914, it arrived in India. Initially it became part of the Jhansi Brigade in the 5th Division of the Indian Army. In December 1915 they moved to Mesopotamia where they became part of 34 Brigade, 18th Division of the Indian Army, and saw action at both Butaniyeh and Nasariyeh. In July 1916 they moved on

Queen's Own (Royal West Kent Regiment) Cap Badge.

to Baghdad where they were involved in the fighting which finally defeated the Turks.

The battalion consisted of eight companies, A to H. The men of Dartford made up 'C' Company which before the war had used the local drill hall by Central Park. The land on which the drill hall was built was donated by Lieutenant Colonel Charles Newman Kidd who had been the commanding officer of the Dartford Volunteer Rifle Corps between 1872 and 1884.

'E' Company of the 1st/5th Battalion comprised men who lived in nearby Sidcup.

During the First World War the regiment managed to raise a total of thirty-one battalions which served and fought in France, Italy, Gallipoli, Salonika, Mesopotamia, Palestine, Egypt, Africa, India and Germany. In doing so they added seventy-three battle honours to their colours, winning four Victoria Crosses along the way, all of which came at a price of the lives of some 8,000 officers and men. The Regimental Memorial that commemorates all those from the regiment who were killed during the First World War, is situated in Brenchley Gardens at Maidstone, Kent.

Queen's Own (Royal West Kent Regiment) Regimental Memorial.

There is also another memorial that was erected in commemoration of the Queen's Own (Royal West Kent Regiment) in the village of Tetre in Belgium, the location of the regiment's first action in the war, at 8.20am on Sunday, 23 August 1914.

There are the names of seventeen soldiers from the Queen's Own (Royal West Kent Regiment) commemorated on the Delhi Memorial (India Gate), two of whom were from the 1st/5th Battalion.

Corporal Albert North (240747) was attached to the Motorised Transport 1st Advanced Repair Shop, Army Service Corps, when he was killed on 25 October 1918, less than three weeks from the date of the Armistice. Although commemorated on the Delhi Memorial, he is actually buried at the Peshawar British Cemetery.

Tetre in Belgium. Queen's Own (Royal West Kent Regiment) War Memorial.

Private Henry Smith (240127) was attached to the 1st Armoured Motor Brigade, HQ Machine Gun Corps (Motors), when he was killed on 1 November 1918. He is also buried at the Peshawar British Cemetery.

There are a further twenty-eight soldiers from the Queen's Own (Royal West Kent Regiment) who are buried at the Gorre British and Indian Cemetery which, despite what its name suggests, is actually to be found in the Pas de Calais region of France.

The Baghdad (North Gate) War Cemetery, in what is today Iraq, has the remains of 177 officers and men of the Queen's Own (Royal West Kent Regiment) buried there. Sixteen of these were from the 1st/5th Battalion.

Private Alfred Henry Cooper (240414), 1st/5th Battalion when he was killed on

Delhi Memorial (India Gate). (Commonwealth War Graves Commission)

30 August 1916 aged 26. He was originally buried in the Yarbashi Cemetery in Asia Minor before being exhumed and brought to his final resting place in Baghdad (North Gate) War Cemetery. His parents, Alfred and Jane Cooper, lived at 23 Treelands, Bromley, Kent.

Private H.W. Curtis (240493), 1st/5th Battalion, was killed on 8 July 1917.

Lance Corporal Herbert Elwood (242017), 1st/5th Battalion, died on 15 November 1918, four days after the Armistice was signed.

Private J.G. Grout (240522), 1st/5th Battalion was killed on 3 October 1916. He was initially buried at Entilly Cemetery in Asia Minor, but his body was exhumed and moved to the Baghdad (North Gate) War Cemetery.

Private Henry William Hague (G/30280), 1st/5th Battalion, was killed on 17 July 1918, aged 40. Henry left a widow, Sophia, who lived at 7 Cambridge Street, Tunbridge Wells.

Private G.J. Harrod was a (240520) in the 1st/5th Battalion when he was killed on 16 October 1916. He was originally buried at the Tarsus Cemetery in Asia Minor, before his body was exhumed and re-buried at the Baghdad (North Gate) War Cemetery.

Baghdad (North Gate) War Cemetery. (Commonwealth War Graves Commission)

Private H.W. Johnson (G/26820) was with the 1st/5th Battalion which had arrived in Mesopotamia, landing at Basra, in December 1917 where they saw action against Turkish forces at Fat-ha Gorge, Little Zab and the Battle of Sharqat. He was 22 years old at the time of his death on 18 October 1918. His parents, William and Jane Johnson, lived at 16 Upper Duke Street, Kettering, Northamptonshire.

Private W. Knight (G/25782), 1st/5th Battalion died on 10 October 1919. He is mentioned on the CWGC website but he does not show up on the First World War British Army Medal Rolls index cards system with just his initial, although there is a direct match to William Knight.

Private E.W. Layer (240710) enlisted at Bromley in Kent, into the 1st/5th Battalion. He was killed on 20 December 1916 and, although he was originally buried at the Afion Kara Hissar Cemetery in Asia Minor, his body was exhumed and brought to the Baghdad (North Gate) War Cemetery.

Private Ernest William Layer arrived in the region on 26 August 1915 as part of the Mesopotamian Expeditionary Force and had a previous army service number of TF/2498. He was awarded the 1914-15 Star, as well as the British War and Victory Medals.

Private George William Pott (2288) was 20 years old and attached to the 2nd Battalion when he died of his wounds whilst being held as a prisoner of war, on 4 June 1916. He was the son of George and Ellen Pott of 8 Frognal Villas, Green Lane, Chislehurst, Kent

Private Walter Isaac Shelley (G/30323), 1st/5th Battalion died on 14 December 1919.

Private William Alexander Tall (2458), 1st/5th Battalion, died on 11 July 1916 whilst being held as a prisoner of war. He was 28 years old. His parents, William and Annie Tall, lived at 7 The Grove, Gravesend, Kent.

Private Henry William Vallins was born in Bromley, Kent in 1887 and prior to enlisting in the army during the First World War he was a domestic gardener by way of occupation. The 1901 Census shows him working as a railway porter.

When he joined up at Bromley on 8 August 1914, he became a

private (1979) in the 1st/5th Battalion. He also served with the 5th and 2nd battalions. When he died on 31 July 1916 he was 32 years of age.

There is an extremely interesting letter attached to Henry's army service record. It is dated 13 April 1918 and was sent from the War Office, Alexandra House, Kingsway, London WC2 to the No. 2 Infantry Record Office at Hounslow.

> *'A postcard, addressed to No. 240466 (1979) L/Cpl. H. Vallins, 1/5th Royal West Kent Regiment, attached 2nd Battalion, Prisoner of War in Turkey, was returned from Turkey with an endorsement to the effect that Vallins was deceased. The relatives were informed that no confirmation of this statement had been received, and that, pending the result of further enquiry, it would not be accepted as correct for official purposes. They should now be informed that enquiries in Turkey have produced no indication that L/Cpl. Vallins is still living; and that, in view of the fact that he has never been reported by the Government of Turkey as having reached any of the internment camps of that country, and has apparently never communicated with his relatives since the fall of Kut, it is feared that there can no longer be any reason to question the accuracy of the endorsement on the returned postcard; and it has, accordingly, been accepted for official purposes.*
>
> *Non-effective documents should now be prepared, the date of death being taken as between 29.4.16 and 29.3.17.'*

The First Battle of Kut began on 5 April 1916 and ended with Britain's unconditional surrender on 29 April 1916. Some 8,000 British and Indian troops were taken prisoner, many of whom were already weak and ill from sickness. Whilst in captivity many of them were treated cruelly and were physically beaten by their Turkish captors. A number of them would also die whilst in captivity as prisoners of war.

His parents, Frederick and Sarah Vallins, were living at 42 Bromley Crescent, Bromley, after the war but at the time of the 1911 Census were at 57 Southlands Road, Bromley, including Henry's sister, Ada. There were other siblings who had already left home by the time of the 1911 Census, George, Sarah, Annie, Matilda and Minnie. George does not appear to have served in the military during the war.

Private George William Vousden (26838), 1st/5th Battalion, was born in Milton in 1894. He was part of the Mesopotamian Expeditionary Force when he died of pneumonia on 5 June 1918 at the age of 24.

After the war his parents, John and Eliza Vousden, lived of 138 High Street, Queensborough, Kent although the 1911 Census showed the family living at 45 Maple Street, Sheerness, Kent. George was the eldest of four children. His brother Frederick was a year younger, with his sisters, Kate and Jessie being 14 and 13 respectively.

Private Frederick Arthur Vousden, enlisted on 21 February 1916 at Maidstone. He was 20 years of age and was a butcher by trade. Like his brother George, he became a private (G/12299) in the Queen's Own (Royal West Kent Regiment) as part of the 7th Battalion.

He arrived in France as part of the British Expeditionary Force on 16 June 1916 and exactly one year later, on 16 July 1917, he suffered a gunshot wound to the head and was recorded as being seriously ill. He was originally treated in hospital in France before returning to England on 31 July 1917.

He was finally discharged from the army on 31 January 1919. His home address at the time is shown as being in Edinburgh, although it is not clear if that is a hospital address where he was still receiving treatment for his injuries.

Frederick died at 51 Mount Pleasant Road, Alton in Hampshire on 16 July 1932 aged 36. In his will he left his entire estate of £801 11 shillings, to his widow, Abby Margaret Vousden.

Private George Edward Wakenell was born in Forrest Hill, London. Not long after he had turned 21 years of age, he became a private (TF/1381) (240157) in the 1st/5th Battalion. He died on 29 October 1916, so it is believed, whilst being held captive in a Turkish prisoner of war camp.

He was the son of Arthur and Priscilla Wakenell, who lived in Beckenham, Kent. They had four other children: two daughters, Dorothy and Louisa as well as two sons: Harry, who was born in 1898, and William who was born on 27 August 1891 in West Wickham.

At the age of 21 William arrived in America, having sailed from Liverpool on 18 October 1912 on board the SS *Corsican*. He arrived in Montreal, Canada on 27 October 1912 and crossed the border into the United States.

He was drafted in to the American Army on 13 May 1918 becoming a private (2377) in the 56th Infantry, 7th Division. His draft card shows that he was a labourer working for the Ford Motor Company at Highlands Park in Michigan. He was demobilized from the army on 13 January 1919. It is not known whether or not he was sent to France on active service.

The 'Draft' was the American version of the British conscription. On the bottom left hand corner of the American Draft Card, it says: 'If person is of African descent, tear off this corner.'

William died on 27 August 1941 aged 49 in Detroit, Michigan and is buried in the city's Grandlawn cemetery.

Private Frederick Hastings Wingrove (240125), 1st/5th Battalion, enlisted at Chatham. He was 21 years of age and the son of Mrs Fanny Elizabeth Williams. The 1911 Census showed the family living at 2 Boundary Road, Chatham. It would appear that he was given the middle name of Hastings for no other reason than that was the town of his birth. He was killed on 31 December 1916 and was originally buried at the Tarsus Cemetery, Asia Minor before his body was exhumed and re-buried at the Baghdad (North Gate) War Cemetery.

Frederick had a brother, Leonard Guy Lewis Wingrove, who was a year younger than he was, as well as a step brother, Lionel Frederick Williams. Leonard also served during the war, enlisting at Chatham on 20 January 1915 aged 19, although by this time the family had moved to 20a Old Road, Chatham. His occupation was shown as that of an outfitter's assistant in the tailoring business. On his enlistment he became a private (51259) in the Royal Army Medical Corps.

Six days later his military service was over when he was 'discharged, not being likely to become an efficient Soldier (Medical Grounds)'. There is no explanation included in what is a very short army service record. Leonard married Ethel G. Winch at Andover, Hampshire in 1943 when he was 46 years of age and died in 1961 at the age of 64.

CHAPTER SIXTEEN

Margaret Maule

In February 2013 an article appeared in the national press about an old suitcase which had been found in a cupboard in Abertay University, Dundee. On opening the suitcase it was found to contain nursing memorabilia dating back to the First World War appertaining to a lady by the name of Margaret Maule who, in 1917, had been a nurse working at the Dartford War Hospital, where she looked after wounded German prisoners of war.

The university's website provided the following information about Margaret. She undertook her nurse training at what was then called Merryflatts Hospital, now the Southern General Hospital, in Glasgow. The training lasted for three years between 1914 and 1917 and on completion she became a nurse with the Queen Alexandra's Nursing Service, and volunteered to serve overseas. Instead of being sent to France or Belgium, however, she was sent to the Dartford War Hospital, or the Lower Southern Hospital Dartford, which treated wounded German prisoners of war. She started work there as a staff nurse on 25 September 1917.

This was ironic for two reasons: firstly because her younger brother John had already been killed in the war, and secondly because there were other hospitals in Dartford that treated Australian and American wounded servicemen. The latter being the Upper Southern Hospital, which adjoined the hospital where she had been sent to work.

Nurse Margaret Maude.

An entry in her diary shows that she initially had reservations about caring for German prisoners of war, feelings which she managed to overcome, allowing her to undertake her work unhindered.

The German prisoners who were sent to the Dartford Hospital were those with very serious wounds and injuries. Records show that 285 of them died whilst being treated there. Initially buried in the grounds of the nearby Darenth Hospital, their remains were moved in 1967 to the national German war cemetery at Cannock Chase in Staffordshire.

It has to be remembered that nursing as a profession was still in its infancy and had only really progressed as far as it had as a result of the second Boer War in South Africa, which took place between 1899 and 1902. The war had shown the need for more nurses as well as ensuring that they were also professionally trained which simply didn't exist at the time. So it was that Queen Alexandra's Imperial Nursing Service came in to existence. Prior to this nurses had been provided by the Army Nursing Service which began in the 1850s during the time of the Crimean War.

When the Lower Southern Hospital in Dartford finally closed its doors to the last of the German PoWs in mid-1919, Margaret resigned her position and moved back to Scotland where she went to work at the Shakespeare Hospital in Glasgow on 1 August 1919. Before the war the hospital had been a school but had been transformed into a hospital to cater for the ever increasing number of wounded British and Allied wounded servicemen.

When she retired in 1969 she was 82 years of age and was living at 46 Dunchurch Road, Oldhall, Paisley. The 1901 Scottish Census shows that Margaret was born in Paisley in 1886 and that along with her parents, David and Margaret Maule, and her two younger brothers, John and Neil, she lived at 5 McKernell Street, Paisley. Her father was a house joiner.

Her brother John was a private (267695) in the 6th (Morayshire) Battalion, Seaforth Highlanders when he was killed in action on 9 April 1917. He was 24 years of age, born in Kinglassie, Fifeshire, before the family had moved to Paisley where he grew up and enlisted in the army early in the war.

The date of John's death on Easter Sunday was also the first day of the Battle of Arras. The 6th Battalion of the Seaforth Highlanders were in the front line trenches at Roclincourt when the whistle blew for them to go over the top at 0530 hours. By the end of the first day's fighting John and ninety-four of his friends and comrades in arms, had lost their lives. John had been with the battalion for two years and had seen some of the bloodiest fighting of the war, including the Battle of the Somme.

Although he had only served with the Seaforth Highlanders his service number had changed three times. It started off as S/2450, was then changed to 5339 and finally ended up as 267695. He first arrived in France with his battalion on 25 March 1915, which besides the British War Medal and the Victory Medal, meant that he was also entitled to the 1915 Star.

6th Battalion, Seaforth Highlanders.

Afterword

I have enjoyed writing and researching this book very much indeed, because just when I begin to think that I cannot be surprised any more I discover a story that truly amazes me.

It has always been difficult to judge yesteryear by today's standards because what we have today is so vastly different, whether in relation to wealth, morals or in people's expectations of life in general; but realistically that is also the only barometer of measure available to us.

For me the beacon of light that still shines brightly from those dark and sometimes depressing days, is the bravery and honour of the young men, no matter what their position in society. Officer and soldier stood side by side in their fight for freedom and justice, and in many cases they died in the same way. God bless them all, and may their memories live on so that it can be seen how brave they were in their quest to secure peace and freedom for future generations.

About the Author

Stephen Wynn is retired having served with Essex Police as a constable for thirty years. He is married to Tanya and has two sons and a daughter.

His interest in history has been fuelled by the fact that both his grandfathers served in and survived the First World War, one with the Royal Irish Rifles, the other in the Mercantile Marine, and his father was a member of the Royal Army Ordnance Corps during the Second

World War. Both Stephen's sons, Luke and Ross, were members of the armed forces, serving five tours of Afghanistan between 2008 and 2013. Both were injured. This led to his first book, *Two Sons in a Warzone – Afghanistan: The True Story of a Father's Conflict* published in October 2010. He has also written three crime thrillers and several books in the Towns & Cities in the Great War series for Pen & Sword.

Sources

Commonwealth War Graves Commission

Ancestry.co.uk

British Newspaper Archive

thetablet.co.uk

The National Archives

www.dartfordarchive.org.uk

www.airfieldinformationexchange.com

www.scotish-places.info

Wikipedia

www.redcross.org.uk

www.greatwar.co.uk

www.1914-1918.invisionzone.com

www.firstworldwar.com

Index